CONTENTS

INTRODUCTION

Since July 2010 the AAT's assessments have fallen within the **Qualifications and Credit Framework** and most papers are now assessed by way of an on demand **computer based assessment**. BPP Learning Media has invested heavily to ensure our ground breaking materials are as relevant as possible for this method of assessment. In particular, our **suite of online resources** ensures that you are prepared for online testing by allowing you to practise numerous online tasks that are similar to the tasks you will encounter in the AAT's assessments.

The BPP range of resources comprises:

- **Texts**, covering all the knowledge and understanding needed by students, with numerous illustrations of 'how it works', practical examples and tasks for you to use to consolidate your learning. The majority of tasks within the texts have been written in an interactive style that reflects the style of the online tasks we anticipate the AAT will set. Texts are available in our traditional paper format and, in addition, as ebooks which can be downloaded to your PC or laptop.

- **Question banks**, including additional learning questions plus the AAT's practice assessment and a number of other full practice assessments. Full answers to all questions and assessments, prepared by BPP Learning Media Ltd, are included. Our Question banks are provided free of charge in an online environment containing tasks similar to those you will encounter in the AAT's testing environment. This means you can become familiar with being tested in an online environment prior to completing the real assessment.

- **Passcards**, which are handy pocket-sized revision tools designed to fit in a handbag or briefcase to enable you to revise anywhere at anytime. All major points are covered in the Passcards which have been designed to assist you in consolidating knowledge.

- **Workbooks**, which have been designed to cover the units that are assessed by way of project/case study. The Workbooks contain many practical tasks to assist in the learning process and also a sample assessment or project to work through.

- **Lecturers' resources**, providing a further bank of tasks, answers and full practice assessments for classroom use, available separately only to lecturers whose colleges adopt BPP Learning Media material. The practice assessments within the Lecturers' resources are available in both paper format and online in e format.

This Text for Basic Accounting I has been written specifically to ensure comprehensive yet concise coverage of the AAT's new learning outcomes and assessment criteria. It is fully up to date as at June 2012 and reflects both the AAT's unit guide and the practice assessments provided by the AAT.

Each chapter contains:

- Clear, step by step explanation of the topic

- Logical progression and linking from one chapter to the next

- Numerous illustrations of 'how it works'

- Interactive tasks within the text of the chapter itself, with answers at the back of the book. In general, these tasks have been written in the interactive form that students can expect to see in their real assessments

- Test your learning questions of varying complexity, again with answers supplied at the back of the book. In general these test questions have been written in the interactive form that students can expect to see in their real assessments

The emphasis in all tasks and test questions is on the practical application of the skills acquired.

If you have any comments about this book, please e-mail paulsutcliffe@bpp.com or write to Paul Sutcliffe, Senior Publishing Manager, BPP Learning Media Ltd, BPP House, Aldine Place, London W12 8AA.

VAT

You will find examples and questions throughout this Text which need you to calculate or be aware of a rate of VAT. This is stated at 20% in these examples and questions.

A NOTE ON TERMINOLOGY

On 1 January 2012, the AAT moved from UK GAAP to IFRS terminology. Although you may be used to UK terminology, you need to now know the equivalent international terminology for your assessments.

The following information is taken from an article on the AAT's website and describes how the terminology changes impact on students studying for each level of the AAT QCF qualification.

What is the impact of IFRS terms on AAT assessments?

The list shown in the table that follows gives the 'translation' between UK GAAP and IFRS.

UK GAAP	IFRS
Final accounts	Financial statements
Trading and profit and loss account	**Income statement or Statement of comprehensive income**
Turnover or Sales	Revenue or Sales Revenue
Sundry income	Other operating income
Interest payable	Finance costs
Sundry expenses	Other operating costs
Operating profit	Profit from operations
Net profit/loss	Profit/Loss for the year/period
Balance sheet	**Statement of financial position**
Fixed assets	Non-current assets
Net book value	Carrying amount
Tangible assets	Property, plant and equipment
Reducing balance depreciation	Diminishing balance depreciation
Depreciation/Depreciation expense(s)	Depreciation charge(s)
Stocks	Inventories
Trade debtors or Debtors	Trade receivables
Prepayments	Other receivables
Debtors and prepayments	Trade and other receivables
Cash at bank and in hand	Cash and cash equivalents
Trade creditors or Creditors	Trade payables

UK GAAP	IFRS
Accruals	Other payables
Creditors and accruals	Trade and other payables
Long-term liabilities	Non-current liabilities
Capital and reserves	Equity (limited companies)
Profit and loss balance	Retained earnings
Minority interest	Non-controlling interest
Cash flow statement	**Statement of cash flows**

This is certainly not a comprehensive list, which would run to several pages, but it does cover the main terms that you will come across in your studies and assessments. However, you won't need to know all of these in the early stages of your studies – some of the terms will not be used until you reach Level 4. For each level of the AAT qualification, the points to bear in mind are as follows:

Level 2 Certificate in Accounting

The IFRS terms do not impact greatly at this level. Make sure you are familiar with 'receivables' (also referred to as 'trade receivables'), 'payables' (also referred to as 'trade payables'), and 'inventories'. The terms sales ledger and purchases ledger – together with their control accounts – will continue to be used. Sometimes the control accounts might be called 'trade receivables control account' and 'trade payables control account'. The other term to be aware of is 'non-current asset' – this may be used in some assessments.

Level 3 Diploma in Accounting

At this level you need to be familiar with the term 'financial statements'. The financial statements comprise an 'income statement' (profit and loss account), and a 'statement of financial position' (balance sheet). In the income statement the term 'revenue' or 'sales revenue' takes the place of 'sales', and 'profit for the year' replaces 'net profit'. Other terms may be used in the statement of financial position – eg 'non-current assets' and 'carrying amount'. However, specialist limited company terms are not required at this level.

Level 4 Diploma in Accounting

At Level 4 a wider range of IFRS terms is needed, and in the case of Financial statements (FNST), are already in use – particularly those relating to limited companies. Note especially that an income statement becomes a 'statement of comprehensive income'.

Note: The information above was taken from an AAT article from the 'assessment news' area of the AAT website (www.aat.org.uk).

ASSESSMENT STRATEGY

Basic Accounting I (BAI) is the first of two financial accounting assessments at level 2. The AAT recommend that BAI is studied and taken before BAII.

The assessment is normally a two hour computer based assessment.

The BAI assessment consists of 16 tasks, six in Section 1 and ten in Section 2.

Once BAI is achieved the following units will be awarded

- Preparing and recording financial documentation
- Processing ledger transactions and extracting a trial balance

The following unit is assessed in both BAI and BAII and will only be awarded once BAI and BAII have been achieved

- Principles of recording and processing financial transactions

Competency

Learners will be required to demonstrate competence in both sections of the assessment. For the purpose of assessment the competency level for AAT assessment is set at 70 per cent. The level descriptor in the table below describes the ability and skills students at this level must successfully demonstrate to achieve competence.

QCF Level descriptor	Summary
	Achievement at level 2 reflects the ability to select and use relevant knowledge, ideas, skills and procedures to complete well-defined tasks and address straightforward problems. It includes taking responsibility for completing tasks and procedures and exercising autonomy and judgement subject to overall direction or guidance.
	Knowledge and understanding ■ Use understanding of facts, procedures and ideas to complete well-defined tasks and address straightforward problems ■ Interpret relevant information and ideas ■ Be aware of the types of information that are relevant to the area of study or work
	Application and action ■ Complete well-defined, generally routine tasks and address straightforward problems ■ Select and use relevant skills and procedures ■ Identify, gather and use relevant information to inform actions ■ Identify how effective actions have been
	Autonomy and accountability ■ Take responsibility for completing tasks and procedures ■ Exercise autonomy and judgement subject to overall direction or guidance

AAT UNIT GUIDE

The purpose of the unit

Basic Accounting I is designed to introduce the candidate to the double entry bookkeeping system and associated documents and processes. The learner is taken to the stage of extracting an initial trial balance, before any adjustments are made.

Learning Objectives

Basic Accounting I will enable candidates to develop an understanding of a manual double entry bookkeeping system.

Candidates will develop the necessary knowledge and skills to deal with documents that are sent to and from organisations, and to code and file those documents appropriately. They will need to know how to make entries in sales, purchases and returns day books, and to transfer those totals, and cash book and petty cash book totals, to the sales, purchases and general ledgers.

Candidates will be able to produce an initial trial balance.

Learning outcomes

Basic Accounting I consists of 12 learning outcomes:

Learning outcome	Covered in Chapters
Understand the role of the books of prime entry	3
Understand the principles of coding	4, 5, 7, 8
Understand the double entry bookkeeping system	6
Understand the various types of discount	2
Prepare the financial documents to be sent to credit customers	1, 4
Enter sales invoices and credit notes into the appropriate books of prime entry	3
Process payments from customers	4
Process suppliers' invoices and credit notes	3
Enter supplier invoices and credit notes into the appropriate books of prime entry	3
Prepare payments to suppliers	5
Process ledger transactions from the books of prime entry	7, 8
Prepare ledger balances and an initial trial balance	6, 9

Delivery guidance

The topics which will be tested are:

1   Books of prime entry: Sales and sales returns day books and Purchases and purchases returns day books, including VAT, and analytical columns where appropriate

- Understanding the purpose, content, format and relationship with the double entry bookkeeping system PRP 1.1, PRP 3.3

- Entering invoices and credit notes into books of prime entry PRF 2.2, 5.2, PRP 1.1, 1.4

- Transferring data from day books to sales, purchases and general ledgers, including control accounts PLT 1.1, PRP 3.4

2   Cash book (with bank, VAT and settlement discount columns)

- Transferring data from the cash book to sales, purchases and general ledgers, including control accounts. Data includes cash sales, cash purchases, discounts received and discounts allowed, payments to suppliers, receipts from customers and other payments and receipts

- The learner will not be required to make entries in the cash book in Basic Accounting I

- Understanding the use of the cash book as part of the double entry system or a book of prime entry PLT 1.2, PRP 3.3, 3.4

3   Petty cash book

- Transferring receipts and expenses from an analysed petty cash book to the general ledger

- The learner will not be required to make entries in the petty cash book in Basic Accounting I

- Understanding the use of the petty cash book as part of the double entry system or a book of prime entry PLT 1.3, PRP 3.3, 3.4

4   Understanding coding within a double entry bookkeeping system

- Coding includes account code, product code and general ledger code

- Understanding the use of coding within a filing system. Coding includes customer code, supplier code, document number PRP 2.1, 2.2

5   Double entry bookkeeping

- Understanding the accounting equation and relationship with the double entry bookkeeping system PRP 3.1, 3.2

- Identifying and understanding capital income and capital expenditure PRP 3.5

- Identifying and understanding revenue income and revenue expenditure PRP 3.6

- Making entries in the sales ledger, purchases ledger and general ledger, including entries in control accounts. Entries include cash sales, cash purchases, discounts received and discounts allowed, payments to suppliers, receipts from customers and other payments and receipts. PRP 3.4 PLT 1.1, 1.2, 1.3

- Balancing ledger accounts PLT 2.1

- Extracting an initial trial balance PLT 2.2

6 Trade, bulk and settlement discounts

- Understanding the reasons for offering discounts

- Understanding the application of discounts

- Understanding the effect of each discount on the VAT calculation PRP 4.1

7 Understanding the purpose and content of petty cash vouchers, invoices, credit notes and remittance advice notes PRP 1.2

8 Preparing and coding sales invoices and credit notes, including trade, bulk and settlement discount(s) and VAT, from quotations, price lists, customer orders, delivery notes or discount policy PRF 1.1, 1.2, 2.1, PRP 1.2, 4.2

9 Preparing statements of account to be sent to trade receivables PRF 1.3 (sic)

10 Checking receipts from customers are accurately calculated and valid against supporting information, and identifying and dealing with discrepancies in amounts, including under/overpayments and taking discounts incorrectly. Supporting information includes the customer remittance advice note, statement of account, sales invoices and the sales ledger PRF 3.1, 3.2

11 Checking supplier invoices and credit notes against purchase orders, goods received notes and delivery notes, including discounts. Identifying discrepancies including non delivery of goods, incorrect goods, incorrect calculations or incorrect discounts. PRF 4.1, 4.2

12 Coding supplier invoices and credit notes PRF 5.1

13 Reconciling supplier statements with the purchases ledger, noting discrepancies PRF 6.1

14 Calculating payments due to suppliers from ledgers and supplier statements PRF 6.2

15 Preparing remittance advice notes PRF 6.3

16 Understanding when authorisation is required PRP 1.3

Note:

This learning area does not require the learner to:

- make entries into the cash book and petty cash book, only to transfer data from those books

- reconcile control accounts, only to make entries to those accounts

- understand or prepare journal entries

These topics will be dealt with in Basic Accounting II.

For assessment purposes sales and purchases ledger control accounts will be contained in the general ledger forming part of the double entry. The terms sales and purchases ledger control accounts will be used throughout the assessment for consistency. The individual accounts of trade receivables and trade payables will be in the sales and purchases ledgers and will therefore be regarded as subsidiary accounts.

chapter 1:
BUSINESS DOCUMENTATION

chapter coverage 📖

This opening chapter briefly introduces the world of business and then looks at the types of business documentation that are encountered. The topics covered are:

✍ Introduction to business

✍ The general types of transaction that businesses have and ways of classifying them

✍ The documents that businesses deal with and record

INTRODUCTION TO BUSINESS

A business exists so that its activities make a PROFIT for its OWNER (the person who has invested money in it). The business makes a profit if its INCOME is more than its EXPENSES. Its activities involve using its ASSETS (items that it owns, such as cash and equipment). In doing so it normally incurs LIABILITIES, which are items that it owes such as loans and overdrafts.

We shall see how these terms link together in more detail in Chapter 6.

The simplest type of business is that of a SOLE TRADER. A sole trader is someone who trades under their own name and who owns the business outright. Many businesses are sole traders, from electricians through to accountants. The owner is not necessarily the only person working in the business as he or she may employ a number of other staff. But, in most cases, the sole trader is in charge of most of the business functions such as buying and selling the goods or performing the services.

The owner of the business is the one who initially contributes money or CAPITAL to the business, although it might also have a LOAN, either commercial or from friends. The owner is also the only one to benefit from the profit of the business, normally by taking money or goods out of the business (known as DRAWINGS).

TYPES OF TRANSACTION

Businesses tend to carry out the same types of business transaction, although on different scales depending on their size.

Typical transactions that businesses will undertake include:

- Selling goods or services
- Buying goods to resell
- Paying money into the bank
- Withdrawing cash from the bank
- Paying expenses from the bank account or from small amounts of cash
- Paying the owner's drawings
- Paying taxes such as VAT

Each and every one of these transactions must be correctly recorded in the business's accounting records, and this is what will be covered in this Text.

The accounting system provides valuable information to the owner:

- How much money is owing to the business and from whom: its customers or TRADE RECEIVABLES

- How much money is owed by the business and to whom: its suppliers or TRADE PAYABLES

- How much money the business holds in hand (PETTY CASH) and in its bank account (BANK)

There is an important distinction to be made at this point between cash and credit transactions.

CASH TRANSACTIONS occur when cash changes hands at the time of the transaction: payment is made or received immediately. These include payments and receipts made:

- In notes and coins (actual cash)
- By cheque, credit card or debit card.

The important factor is the timing of the payment. No trade receivables or trade payables are involved in a cash transaction. The primary documentation created for this type of transaction is a TILL RECEIPT.

CREDIT TRANSACTIONS occur when the goods or services are given or received now but it is agreed that payment will be made or received at a future date after a period of credit. Credit transactions involve the issue or receipt of an INVOICE and the creation of a trade receivable or a trade payable for the amount outstanding. When the amount is finally paid over, this may be in the form of cash or a cheque, card or automated payment.

Task 1

Tara sells goods to Cathy for £100 and they agree Cathy will pay Tara in cash in two weeks' time. This is (tick ONE)

a cash transaction	
a credit transaction	

THE PURPOSE OF ACCOUNTING

The basic purpose of ACCOUNTING is to record and classify accurately the business's transactions.

It is the business's documentation that contains details of its transactions, so the information on these documents must be complete, accurate and properly checked.

We shall cover these processes in this Text, but first we need to get more of an insight into what businesses actually do, and how this is reflected in the types of information found on business documents. We shall therefore look initially at four key pieces of business documentation, each of which is designed to allow accurate recording. These are:

- Invoices
- Credit notes
- Remittance advice notes
- Petty cash vouchers

INVOICES

The primary business document that relates to credit transactions is the invoice. This is given by the seller to the buyer. For the seller it is a sales invoice and for the buyer the same document is a purchase invoice.

An invoice is a request for payment for the goods or services that have been sold and it details precisely how much is due and when.

HOW IT WORKS

Here is an example, for a credit transaction in which a buyer or customer (Whitehill Superstores) purchases six dishwashers from a seller or supplier (Southfield Electrical). The supplier has agreed that the buyer only has to pay 30 days after taking the goods. This 30 days is the period of credit which distinguishes the sale as a credit sale rather than a cash sale. The period is called '30 days credit'.

INVOICE	Invoice number 56314		
Southfield Electrical **Industrial Estate** **Benham DR6 2FF** **Tel: 01239 345639**			
VAT registration:	0264 2274 49		
Date/tax point:	7 September 20XX		
Order number:	32011		
Customer:	Whitehill Superstores 28 Whitehill Park Benham DR6 5LM		
Account number (customer code)	SL 44		
Description/product code	**Quantity**	**Unit amount £**	**Total £**
Zanpoint dishwashers /4425	6	200.00	1,200.00
Net total			1,200.00
VAT at 20%			240.00
Invoice total			1,440.00
Terms 30 days net			

Let's look at the details of the invoice from the supplier (Southfield Electrical) to the buyer (Whitehill Superstores):

- It shows the supplier's name, address and VAT registration number (VAT will be considered in more detail in Chapter 2)

- It has its own unique, sequential document number or code (56314), which allows it to be identified easily (it is much more accurate to refer to 'Invoice 56314' rather than 'the invoice we sent the other day')

- The date of the invoice (also known as the tax point) is important information for Whitehill. It allows Whitehill to see when the invoice is due for payment – in this case 30 days after the invoice date

- The account number or customer code is another example of coding in accounting. Eventually Southfield will have to enter this invoice into its accounting records and this shows exactly which account relates to Whitehill

- The details of the goods are included both in words and by using its product code

- The price of the dishwashers, excluding VAT, as quoted to Whitehill is shown per unit. To find the total price the quantity is multiplied by the unit price to arrive at the net total of the invoice. To this must be added VAT charged at 20%. The resulting invoice total is the amount that Whitehill must pay

- The term "30 days net" shows that payment of the invoice total is due 30 days after the invoice date

Task 2

Tara agrees to sell goods to Cathy for £100 and they agree Cathy will pay Tara in two weeks' time. The business document that Tara should send to Cathy to record this agreement is (tick ONE)

an invoice	
a receipt	

CREDIT NOTES

Another key document is the CREDIT NOTE, which is used to show that the buyer owes less money to the supplier than was originally agreed. Credit notes can be used:

- In credit transactions to reduce an amount that has already been invoiced, so the buyer pays the net amount (the invoice less the credit note)

- In cash transactions when the supplier does not want to refund cash to the buyer but is willing to acknowledge that it owes the buyer some money

HOW IT WORKS

Suppose that one of the dishwashers supplied by Southfield is damaged. When the damaged dishwasher is returned to Southfield, it should issue a CREDIT NOTE to Whitehill which reverses the part of the sales invoice that relates to the damaged dishwasher.

CREDIT NOTE	Credit note number 08641
Southfield Electrical **Industrial Estate** **Benham DR6 2FF** **Tel: 01239 345639**	
VAT registration:	0264 2274 49
Date/tax point:	12 September 20XX
Order number:	32011
Customer:	Whitehill Superstores 28 Whitehill Park Benham DR6 5LM
Account number (customer code)	SL 44

Description/product code	Quantity	Unit amount £	Total £
Zanpoint dishwasher /4425 Reason for credit note: Delivered damaged	1	200.00	200.00

Net total	200.00
VAT at 20%	40.00
Credit note total	240.00
Terms 30 days net	

The credit note is almost identical to an invoice. The only differences are:

- It is described as a credit note
- It has a unique, sequential credit note number rather than an invoice number
- A reason for the credit is noted at the bottom of the credit note

To make sure that buyers do not get invoices and credit notes mixed up, credit notes are often printed in red.

Task 3

Cathy is not happy with her goods when she receives them and Tara agrees that they are not quite of the required standard, so she will only expect payment of £80 rather than £100 at the due time. The business document that Tara should send to Cathy to record this is (tick ONE)

an invoice	
a credit note	

REMITTANCE ADVICE NOTES

When the buyer pays the supplier in a credit transaction, a variety of payment methods may be used, such as a cheque, a debit card or an automated payment from the buyer's bank account to the supplier's. To let the supplier know which invoices are being paid, and which credit notes are being deducted (or netted off), the buyer usually sends the supplier a REMITTANCE ADVICE NOTE which contains that information.

HOW IT WORKS

Suppose that on 20 September Whitehill Superstores has decided to pay Southfield Electrical by cheque what it owed to the company at the beginning of September, which was for invoice 56019 for £316.40 received on 21 August less credit note number 08613 for £47.46 received on 28 August. Along with the cheque it sends the supplier the following remittance advice note.

REMITTANCE ADVICE NOTE	Remittance advice note number
Whitehill Superstores	0937498
28 Whitehill Park	
Benham DR6 5LM	
Supplier:	**Southfield Electrical**
	Industrial Estate
	Benham DR6 2FF
Account number (supplier code)	**PL 526**

Date	Transaction reference	Amount £
21/08/XX	Invoice 56019	316.40
28/08/XX	Credit note 08613	(47.46)
20/09/XX	Payment made - cheque enclosed	268.94

Note that this remittance advice note:

- Is described as a remittance advice note

- Has a unique, sequential remittance advice note number

- Is going from the buyer to the supplier so instead of a customer code it contains a supplier code

- Deducts the amount of the credit note from the amount of the invoice to arrive at the amount of the payment made – though it could contain other invoices or credit notes, and other reductions in the amount owed (especially discounts, which we shall see in Chapter 2)

Task 4

Cathy sends a cheque to Tara for £80 and wishes to make it clear that both the invoice and the credit note are being settled by means of this payment. To clarify this matter for Tara, Cathy should send her (tick ONE)

an invoice	
a credit note	
a remittance advice note	

PETTY CASH VOUCHERS

We noted above that businesses will often have to pay expenses from small amounts of cash held on the premises in a box, known as PETTY CASH. The key document for the proper functioning of a petty cash system is the PETTY CASH VOUCHER, which must be completed and authorised before any cash can be paid out of the petty cash box.

HOW IT WORKS

Suppose that Lara Moschetta, an employee in Southfield Electrical, is sent out by her boss, Trish Epstein, one day to Riseworth Stationers to buy some stationery for use in the administrative office. Lara pays the shop £48 with her own cash (this includes £8 VAT) and understandably wants Southfield Electrical to pay her back. She should therefore get Trish to authorise the Riseworth till receipt, give the authorised receipt to the accountant and then receive her £48 in cash. The accountant will prepare the following petty cash voucher for the expenditure to place in the petty cash box once the £48 has been paid out:

Petty Cash Voucher	Number 067
Date prepared:	12/09/XX
Expenditure	Amount £
Stationery (till receipt attached)	40.00
VAT at 20%	8.00
Total	48.00
Supporting documentation:	
Till receipt dated 12/09/XX	
Cash paid to Lara Moschetta	
Receipt authorised by Trish Epstein	

There are a number of important points to note about this petty cash voucher:

- It has a sequential number, which ensures that all petty cash vouchers are accounted for

- The details of the expense are clear and an authorised receipt is attached

- The amount of the expense is shown (£48 – £8 = £40) plus the VAT of £8

- The voucher is signed by the person claiming the petty cash (Lara Moschetta)

- The voucher shows that the receipt was authorised by an appropriate member of staff

We shall see much more about petty cash vouchers in Basic Accounting II.

Task 5

The document that is used to record payments out of petty cash is (tick ONE)

an petty cash voucher	
an invoice	
a till receipt	

CODING SYSTEMS

We noted above that sales invoices generally have a customer code on them to denote the particular customer in question, and similarly communications with buyers have a supplier code on them. The use of CODING SYSTEMS in an organisation is designed to ensure that:

- information can be recorded accurately and in a timely manner
- documents can be filed and retrieved efficiently

Each organisation will have its own coding system, designed to help it run its processes in the most efficient manner. The system may be:

- Numeric, so that all documents are given a sequential code number or DOCUMENT NUMBER, with the most recent document being given the document number that immediately follows the one before. Different types of document, for example sales invoices and purchase orders, are part of different numbering systems

- Alpha-numeric, so that there is an initial run of letters that tells us something about the items being coded, and then a sequential numeric system as well. The numeric run follows the same principles as for document numbers, and the alpha run may denote:

  - the part of the accounting system in which the document will be recorded

  - the first few letters of a product, supplier, customer or employee name

  - the first few letters of some other classification

HOW IT WORKS

In the case of Southfield Electrical, we saw that the customer code on its invoice was 'SL 44'. An alpha-numeric coding system has been used to create a customer code for its sales invoices:

- The 'alpha' part is SL, which stands for 'Sales Ledger', part of the accounting system for credit customers which we shall come back to in later chapters. All customer codes for credit customers of Southfield Electrical will have this prefix.

- The 'numeric' part is 44, which is the unique part of the code. This will have been allocated because at the time when Whitehill Superstores became a customer, Southfield had allocated 43 customer codes and so Whitehill was given the 44th.

The invoice document number however was 56314, a simple numeric code (the next invoice issued will be 56315), and the credit note document number was 08641 (so the next one issued will be 08642).

In the case of Whitehill Superstores, it used a numeric system for coding its remittance advice note (0937498) and an alpha-numeric system for its supplier code (PL 526, in which 'PL' stands for 'purchases ledger', a record we shall come back to in a later chapter).

Using coding systems

A coding system has two main purposes:

- It allows information to be included in documents in an abbreviated manner, saving time and making the document more user-friendly

- It facilitates filing of documents: sequentially numbered invoices, for instance, can be filed in number order so they are easier to find, and a copy can also be filed in customer code order so it is easy to find all invoices sent to a particular customer. This makes it much easier to deal with enquiries related to that document

As with anything to do with accounting in particular and business transactions in general, it is very important that coding systems are applied carefully and consistently in practice. Most computerised accounting systems, for instance, rely on the accurate use of coding systems.

Task 6

An organisation codes all invoices received from suppliers with a supplier code. A selection of the codes used is given below:

Supplier	Supplier code
Benson Ltd	BEN41
Immer plc	IMM56
Presley Co	PRE62

The organisation has received an invoice from Presley Co. What supplier code should it use for the invoice?

✓	Supplier code
	BEN41
	IMM56
	PRE62

CHAPTER OVERVIEW

- A business's transactions can be categorised as either cash or credit transactions

- An invoice is used in credit transactions to record how much is owed and when it should be paid

- A credit note is used in credit transactions to record that less is owed than was originally invoiced, and in cash transactions to record that the business still owes some money back to a customer

- A remittance advice note is used in credit transactions to help the business receiving the advice note identify which invoices etc are being paid

- A petty cash voucher is used to record payments of petty cash

- Coding systems are used to ensure accuracy of recording and filing

Keywords

Profit – the excess of income over expenses made by a business

Owner – the person who has invested money in the business

Income – what the business earns when it makes sales of goods or services to other parties

Expenses – what the business spends to purchase goods or services for the company

Assets – something that a business owns

Liabilities – something that a business owes

Sole trader – a business that is owned and run by an individual

Capital – the amount of money invested by the owner in the business

Loan – the amount of money invested in a business by a person who is not its owner

Drawings – amounts taken out of the business by the owner

Trade receivable – someone who owes money to the business

Trade payable – someone to whom the business owes money

Petty cash – small amounts of cash held physically within the business

Bank – amounts of money held for the business by its bank

Cash transactions – transactions whereby payment happens at the same time as goods/services are exchanged

Till receipt – the primary documentation for a sale or purchase in cash

Credit transactions – transactions whereby payment is to be made at some future date

Invoice – a document that clearly sets out what money is owed by a named trade receivable to a named trade payable in respect of particular goods or services

Accounting – the process by which a business's transactions are recorded and classified

Credit note – a document that clearly sets out reductions in the amount owed by a trade receivable to a trade payable

Remittance advice note – a document setting out exactly how a payment is made up (ie the invoices/credit notes that it is paying/netting off)

Petty cash – small amounts of cash held on the premises to cover day-to-day expenses

Petty cash voucher – a document that records payments out of petty cash

Coding systems – are used to ensure accuracy of filing and recording

Document number – the unique number allocated from a sequence to a particular document as part of the organisation's coding system

TEST YOUR LEARNING

Test 1

For each of the following transactions determine whether it should be classified as a cash or credit transaction.

	Cash ✓	Credit ✓
Purchase of a van with an agreed payment date in one month's time		
Sale of goods by credit card in a shop		
Purchase of computer disks by cheque		
Purchase of computer disks which are accompanied by an invoice		
Sale of goods which are paid for by cheque		

Test 2

For each of the following transactions, indicate the primary business document that will be created by drawing an arrow from each of the four boxes on the left to one of the boxes on the right.

Sale of goods for cash		Credit note
Return of goods purchased on credit		Remittance advice note
Reimbursement of employee for expense by cash		Invoice
Indication of which amounts that are owed are being paid		Till receipt
		Cheque
		Petty cash voucher

Test 3

Complete the following sentences by deleting one option in each case:

- Where income is more than expenses a business makes a profit/loss

- Where expenses are more than income a business makes a profit/loss

- Bank loans and overdrafts are examples of assets/liabilities

- Cash and trade receivables are example of assets/liabilities

- When a business owner contributes money to the business, this is known as capital/drawings

- When a business owner takes out money from the business, this is known as capital/drawings

chapter 2:
DISCOUNTS AND VAT

chapter coverage 📖

This chapter considers two very important aspects of the transactions that businesses make: discounts and VAT. The topics covered are:

✍ Value added tax (VAT) and its operation

✍ VAT calculations on invoices

✍ Trade, bulk and settlement discounts

✍ The VAT implications of a settlement discount

VAT

We saw on the invoice, credit note and petty cash voucher in Chapter 1 that VALUE ADDED TAX (or VAT) is an issue for businesses that buy and sell. But what is VAT?

VAT is due to HM Revenue and Customs (HMRC) on many goods and services that are sold. It is a tax that is paid by the final consumer but is collected along the way by each seller in the supply chain.

VAT registration

If the sales of a business exceed a certain amount for a year, then a business must register for VAT with HMRC. This means that they have a VAT registration number which, as we saw in Chapter 1, must be included on invoices, credit notes and other business documents.

It also means that the business must charge VAT on all of its sales (known as 'taxable supplies'). This is usually at the STANDARD RATE of 20%. VAT charged on sales is known as OUTPUT TAX.

There is however a benefit, in that the VAT that the business pays when buying from suppliers or paying expenses can be recovered back from HMRC. This is known as INPUT TAX.

Usually every three months the business must complete a VAT return showing the output and input tax. The excess of output tax over input tax must be paid to HMRC. However, if the input tax exceeds the output tax then a refund is due from HMRC.

Task 1

Complete the following sentences:

Output tax is VAT on	purchases
	sales
Input tax is VAT on	purchases
	sales

RATES OF VAT

The standard VAT rate of 20% applies to most items that are bought and sold but some items (such as food and children's clothing) are ZERO-RATED for VAT purposes. This means that the seller of these items charges VAT at 0% (ie no VAT) on his sales. However, if he is charged VAT by his suppliers on his expenses and purchases he can reclaim the input VAT from HMRC.

Other items (such as postal services and rail travel) are EXEMPT from VAT ie no VAT is charged. A seller who makes exempt supplies also does not charge VAT on his sales. The difference is that he is unable to reclaim any input VAT charged on his expenses and purchases.

VAT CALCULATIONS

VAT must be calculated accurately. The rule is that, if the VAT calculation comes up with a figure of more than two decimal places, you always round VAT down to the nearest penny.

The two main calculations that you might be required to make are:

- Calculating VAT on a sales price (the net total)
- Calculating VAT from an invoice total (known as the gross amount)

We shall look at these in turn.

HOW IT WORKS

On the invoice from Southfield Electrical to Whitehill Superstores in Chapter 1, we saw the sale of six dishwashers with a total sales price of £1,200 by a business that had a VAT registration number and that therefore had to charge output VAT.

The net total of the invoice was £1,200.00, so the VAT was calculated as 20% of £1,200.00. This means that the fraction 20/100 is to be applied to £1,200.00.

VAT to be charged = £1,200.00 × 20/100 = £240.00

There is no need to round the amount.

Note the fraction of 20/100 can also be expressed as 1/5 – so all you have to do is divide the net total by 5 to get the VAT:

VAT = £1,200.00/5 = £240.00

Task 2

If the net amount of an invoice is £230.00 then the output VAT is:

£ _____

HOW IT WORKS

Suppose, however, that you are only told the VAT-inclusive invoice total (or gross amount) – a situation that arises quite often in the case of a small purchase from a shop.

If the total of the price of goods plus the VAT is £70.50, how much VAT is included in this price and what is the net total for the goods?

This time the £70.50 includes 20% VAT and therefore to find the VAT part of that, the fraction 20/120 must be applied to the gross amount.

VAT = £70.50 × 20/120 = £11.75

Therefore the net total for the goods is £70.50 – £11.75 = £58.75.

Note the fraction of 20/120 can also be expressed as 1/6 – so all you have to do is divide the gross total by 6 to get the VAT:

VAT = £70.50/6 = £11.75

Task 3

If the invoice total is £246.00 then the output tax is:

£ _____

DISCOUNTS

When selling goods or services a business usually has a standard or LIST PRICE that it charges to all its customers. However, the business may not always charge all customers the full list price of the goods or services – the business may choose to offer a DISCOUNT. There are three types of discount that we must consider:

- Trade discount
- Bulk discount
- Settlement discount

Trade discount

A TRADE DISCOUNT is a percentage reduction from the list price of goods or services. This reduced price may be offered because:

- The customer is regular and valued, or
- As an incentive to a new customer to buy, or
- The customer is in the same trade as the supplier and the supplier wants
- To develop good relations.

The amount of the trade discount will be shown on the face of the invoice as a deduction from the list price before arriving at the net total.

HOW IT WORKS

Continuing with Southfield Electrical and Whitehill Superstores, suppose now that the initial price quotation from Southfield was the list price of £200 per dishwasher but Whitehill were to be allowed a trade discount of 10%.

The invoice would now appear as follows:

INVOICE	Invoice number 56314		
Southfield Electrical **Industrial Estate** **Benham DR6 2FF** **Tel: 01239 345639**			
VAT registration:	0264 2274 49		
Date/tax point:	7 September 20XX		
Order number:	32011		
Customer:	Whitehill Superstores 28 Whitehill Park Benham DR6 5LM		
Account number (customer code)	SL 44		
Description/product code	**Quantity**	**Unit amount** **£**	**Total** **£**
Zanpoint dishwashers /4425 Less: Trade discount 10%	6	200.00	1,200.00 (120.00)
Net total			1,080.00
VAT at 20%			216.00
Invoice total			1,296.00
Terms 30 days net			

This is how the calculations were made:

Step 1   Calculate the total price before the discount by multiplying the quantity by the list price:

$$6 \times £200 = £1,200.00$$

Step 2   Calculate the trade discount as 10% of this total list price:

$$£1,200.00 \times 10\% \ (10/100) = £120.00$$

Step 3   Deduct the trade discount from the total list price to reach the invoice net total:

£1,200.00 – £120.00 = £1,080.00

Step 4   Calculate the VAT at 20% of the invoice net total:

£1,080.00 × 20% (20/100) = £216.00

Step 5   Calculate the invoice total by adding the VAT to the net total:

£1,080.00 + £216.00 = £1,296.00

Task 4

Goods with a list price of £2,400.00 are to be sent to a customer. The customer is allowed a trade discount of 15% and VAT is to be charged at 20%. What is the invoice total?

£ [   ]

Bulk discount

A BULK DISCOUNT is also a percentage reduction from the list price of goods or services, offered because the customer's order is large. The business will offer this to encourage customers to place large orders so costs of administration and delivery are reduced.

Like the trade discount, the amount of the bulk discount will be shown on the face of the invoice as a deduction from the list price before arriving at the net total. It may be offered as well as or instead of a trade discount.

If a bulk discount is offered in addition to a trade discount, it is normal practice to calculate the bulk discount on the amount after trade discount has been deducted.

HOW IT WORKS

Suppose now that as well as a trade discount of 10% Southfield Electrical were also to offer Whitehill Superstores a 5% discount on orders over £1,000 net of trade discount.

The invoice would now appear as follows.

INVOICE	Invoice number 56314
Southfield Electrical **Industrial Estate** **Benham DR6 2FF** **Tel: 01239 345639**	
VAT registration:	0264 2274 49
Date/tax point:	7 September 20XX
Order number:	32011
Customer:	Whitehill Superstores 28 Whitehill Park Benham DR6 5LM
Account number (customer code)	SL 44

Description/product code	Quantity	Unit amount £	Total £
Zanpoint dishwashers /4425	6	200.00	1,200.00
Less: Trade discount 10%			(120.00) 1,080.00
Less: Bulk discount 5%			(54.00)

Net total	1,026.00
VAT at 20%	205.20
Invoice total	1,231.20
Terms 30 days net	

This is how the calculations were made:

Step 1   Calculate the total price less trade discount as before:

£1,200.00 − £120.00 = £1,080.00

Step 2   As this is over the £1,000.00 limit we calculate and deduct the bulk discount at 5% to arrive at the net total:

£1,080.00 – £(1,080.00 × 5/100) = £1,026.00

Step 3   Calculate the VAT at 20% of the invoice net total:

£1,026.00 × 20% (20/100) = £205.20

Step 4   Calculate the invoice total by adding the VAT to the net total:

£1,026.00 + £205.20 = £1,231.20

Task 5

Goods with a list price of £2,400.00 are to be sent to a customer. The customer is allowed a trade discount of 10% and a bulk discount of 12% for orders of £2,000 and over after trade discount has been deducted. VAT is to be charged at 20%. What is the invoice total?

£ [   ]

Settlement discount

A SETTLEMENT DISCOUNT is a percentage discount of the total invoice value that is offered to a customer to encourage that customer to pay or settle the invoice earlier. For example, if it is normal policy to request that payment is made by customers 30 days after the invoice date, a settlement discount of 4% might be offered for payment within ten days of the invoice date.

A settlement discount differs from a trade or bulk discount in that although the seller offers the discount to the customer it is up to the customer to decide whether or not to accept the offer of the discount. Therefore the discount does not appear on the face of the invoice. Instead it is noted at the bottom of the invoice in the "Terms" section.

We also need to consider how to calculate the VAT on an invoice where a settlement discount is offered. If a settlement discount is offered the rule is that:

- the VAT is always calculated on the assumption that the settlement discount is taken up by the customer, and therefore
- the VAT calculation is based on the net invoice total **after deducting** the settlement discount.
- the VAT figure is not adjusted even if the settlement discount is not taken

HOW IT WORKS

Continuing with Southfield and Whitehill, suppose now that Southfield not only offers the 10% trade discount and 5% bulk discount but also a 4% settlement discount for settlement within ten days of the invoice date.

This is what the invoice would look like:

INVOICE	Invoice number 56314		
Southfield Electrical **Industrial Estate** **Benham DR6 2FF** **Tel: 01239 345639**			
VAT registration:	0264 2274 49		
Date/tax point:	7 September 20XX		
Order number:	32011		
Customer:	Whitehill Superstores 28 Whitehill Park Benham DR6 5LM		
Account number (customer code)	SL 44		
Description/product code	**Quantity**	**Unit amount £**	**Total £**
Zanpoint dishwashers /4425	6	200.00	1,200.00
Less: Trade discount 10%			(120.00)
			1,080.00
Less: Bulk discount 5%			(54.00)
Net total			1,026.00
VAT at 20%			196.99
Invoice total			1,222.99
Terms 4% settlement discount for payment within 10 days, otherwise 30 days net			

Now let's look at the calculations involved here. The figures are exactly the same as on the previous invoice until the VAT section is reached. So we will now look at how to calculate the VAT.

Step 1   Calculate the amount of the settlement discount offered by finding 4% of the net invoice total:

$$£1,026.00 \times 4\% (4/100) = £41.04$$

Step 2   In a working, deduct the settlement discount from the net invoice total:

$$£1,026.00 - £41.04 = £984.96$$

Step 3   Calculate the VAT at 20% on the invoice total minus the settlement discount:

$$£984.96 \times 20\% (20/100) = £196.99 \text{ (remember to round down to the nearest penny)}$$

Step 4   Add this VAT amount into the net invoice total to arrive at the total invoice amount:

$$£1,026.00 + £196.99 = £1,222.99$$

Step 5   State the terms of the settlement discount at the bottom of the invoice.

Task 6

Goods with a net invoice total of £368.00 are to be sold to a customer and the customer is offered a 3% settlement discount for payment received within 14 days of the invoice date. What is the invoice total?

£ [ ]

CHAPTER OVERVIEW

- Most businesses will be registered for VAT and must therefore add VAT at 20%, the standard rate, to the list price of the goods or services charged to the customer on the invoice

- From a net total, calculate standard rate VAT at 20/100 or 1/5 of the net amount

- From a gross total, calculate standard rate VAT at 20/120 or 1/6 of the gross amount

- The seller may offer the customer a trade discount, a bulk discount and/or a settlement discount

- Trade and bulk discounts are reductions of list price and are shown on the face of the invoice

- A settlement discount is offered to the customer who may or may not take up the offer, and is shown at the bottom of the invoice as part of the terms

- The amount of the settlement discount must be deducted from the net total of the invoice when calculating VAT, but VAT is then added to the unadjusted net invoice total

Keywords

VAT – a tax levied by HM Revenue and Customs which must be added to the selling price of goods and services at all stages in the production process, paid over to HMRC at each stage of the process and borne by the final consumer

Standard rate of VAT – is 20%

Output tax – VAT on sales

Input tax – VAT on purchases and expenses

Zero rated – sellers of zero-rated items charge 0% on their sales

Exempt – no VAT is charged (but unlike zero-rated supplies the seller is unable to reclaim input VAT)

Trade discount – a percentage discount off the list price of goods and services offered to some long-standing customers or participants in the same trade, or as an incentive to new customers

Bulk discount – a percentage discount off the list price of goods and services offered once an order over a certain size has been placed. Designed to encourage large orders

Keywords cont'd

Settlement discount – a percentage discount off the net invoice total offered in order to provide an incentive to pay the invoice amount early

TEST YOUR LEARNING

Test 1

A business sells 400 items to its customer for £30 per item. Trade discount of 5% is offered, plus a bulk discount of 10% for orders after trade discount of £1,000 or more. No settlement discount is offered.

What is the net amount on the invoice?

£ [   ]

Test 2

(a) A sale is made for £378.00 plus VAT. How much VAT should be charged?

£ [   ]

(b) A sale is made for £378.00 including VAT. How much VAT has been charged and what is the net amount of the sale?

VAT	£	
Net amount	£	

Test 3

For each of the following VAT-inclusive (gross) amounts, calculate the VAT and the net amount.

VAT-inclusive amount	VAT	Net amount
(a) £3,154.80	£	£
(b) £446.40	£	£
(c) £169.20	£	£

Test 4

(a) A customer is purchasing 23 items each with a list price of £56.00. A trade discount of 15% is given to this customer.

Calculate:

(i) Total cost before discount	£	
(ii) Discount	£	
(iii) Net total	£	
(iv) VAT	£	
(v) Invoice total	£	

(b) Suppose that a settlement discount of 3% is also offered. Calculate the same figures on this basis.

(i) Total cost before discount	£	
(ii) Discount	£	
(iii) Net total	£	
(iv) VAT	£	
(v) Invoice total	£	

chapter 3:
THE BASICS OF ACCOUNTING

---

chapter coverage 📖

In this chapter we will consider the basics of recording business transactions in the accounting records. The topics covered are:

✍ Books of prime entry

✍ The Sales Day Book

✍ The sales ledger

✍ The Sales Returns Day Book

✍ The Purchases Day Book

✍ The purchases ledger

✍ The Purchases Returns Day Book

✍ The Cash Book for receipts and payments from the bank account

✍ The Petty Cash Book

BOOKS OF PRIME ENTRY

In the previous two chapters we have looked at some of the basic transactions of a business. We are now ready to start recording some of these transactions in the business's accounting system.

The first stage of the accounting process is to enter details of transaction documents into BOOKS OF PRIME ENTRY. These books of prime entry are often known as DAY BOOKS as, in theory at least, they would be written up every day.

TRANSACTION ➡ BOOKS OF
DOCUMENTS   PRIME ENTRY

We are concerned first with invoices and credit notes, which we shall record in the records of the business making the sale.

INVOICES AND THE SALES DAY BOOK

All of the business's sales invoices sent to credit customers for a period are initially recorded in its book of prime entry which is known as the SALES DAY BOOK.

HOW IT WORKS

A typical Sales Day Book looks like this:

Date 20XX	Customer	Invoice number	Customer code	Invoice total £	VAT £	Net £
1 May	Grigsons Ltd	10356	SL21	199.20	33.20	166.00
1 May	Hall & Co	10357	SL05	105.60	17.60	88.00
1 May	Harris & Sons	10358	SL17	120.00	20.00	100.00
2 May	Jaytry Ltd	10359	SL22	309.60	51.60	258.00

The writing-up of the Sales Day Book for these four transactions has the following steps:

Step 1   Gather the invoices that have been sent out to the customers since the day book was last written up and check that there are no invoices missing (the invoice numbers should be in sequence). All the information needed to enter into the Sales Day Book is on the face of each invoice.

Step 2 Enter the dates of the invoices, the names of the customers and the invoice numbers in the appropriate columns of the day book.

Step 3 The customer code column is also sometimes headed up 'reference' or 'folio'. This is the column where the account numbers for the customers are entered from the face of the invoices. As we saw in Chapter 1, the customer code is the account number given to the customers in the sales ledger (which we will come back to shortly) and therefore is often given the prefix 'SL'. Accuracy and consistency in using this code is important as it helps with the eventual entry of the figures into the accounts.

Step 4 Only three figures are entered from the invoices:

- The invoice total column contains the invoice total including VAT

- The VAT is the amount shown on the face of the invoice

- The net column is the net total (before VAT) on the face of the invoice.

Task 1

An invoice shows the following amounts. Which columns in the Sales Day Book would each amount appear in? Tick ONE box for each amount.

	£	Invoice total	VAT	Net
Goods total	1,236.00			
VAT	247.20			
Total	1,483.20			

THE SALES LEDGER

For each individual credit customer the business needs to keep a record of how much that customer owes to the business at any one time. The way this is done is to record each invoice total in the customer's LEDGER ACCOUNT in the SALES LEDGER. The sales ledger is a record that contains ledger accounts for every credit customer. As we saw in Chapter 1, credit customers which owe money to the business are also known as TRADE RECEIVABLES.

Each credit customer's ledger account contains two sides:

- On the **left-hand side** we record invoices, which **increase** the amount owed by the customer

- On the **right-hand side** we record credit notes, settlement discounts and payments received from the customer, all of which **decrease** the amount owed by the customer

HOW IT WORKS

Step 1   Find the individual customer's account in the sales ledger using the customer code.

Step 2   Enter the **invoice total**, which is the amount the customer actually owes, on the left-hand side of this account.

Step 3   In the 'details' section next to the amount, enter '**SDB**' followed by the **invoice number**. If there is space denoted by 'Date' you should also write in the date.

Looking back at the four invoices entered in the Sales Day Book, they would be entered in the sales ledger as follows.

Sales ledger

	Grigsons Ltd		SL 21
Details	£	Details	£
SDB – 10356	199.20		

	Hall & Co		SL 05
Details	£	Details	£
SDB – 10357	105.60		

Harris & Sons		**SL 17**
Details	£	Details	£
SDB – 10358	120.00		

Jaytry Ltd		**SL 22**
Details	£	Details	£
SDB – 10359	309.60		

We enter the invoice number for each entry as this will be useful when dealing with customer enquiries.

CREDIT NOTES AND THE SALES RETURNS DAY BOOK

Just as invoices are initially entered in their own book of prime entry, so too are credit notes – in the SALES RETURNS DAY BOOK. This looks very similar to the Sales Day Book with the same details being entered.

HOW IT WORKS

A typical Sales Returns Day Book would look like this:

Date 20XX	Customer	Credit note number	Customer code	Credit note total £	VAT £	Net £
4 May	Grigsons Ltd	CN668	SL21	72.00	12.00	60.00
5 May	Harris & Sons	CN669	SL17	96.00	16.00	80.00

The only difference here is that the credit note number is entered rather than an invoice number. Again, all of the details required can be found on the face of the credit note that is used to write up the day book.

Now we must enter each individual credit note in the customer's account in the sales ledger. The amount to be used is the credit note total and this must be entered in the **right-hand side** of the ledger account as it **decreases** how much the customer owes us.

Step 1 Find the individual customer's account in the sales ledger using the customer code.

Step 2 Enter the credit note total, which is the amount of the reduction in what the customer actually owes, on the right-hand side of this account.

Step 3 In the 'details' section next to the amount, enter '**SRDB**' followed by the **credit note number** (and the date if required).

Sales ledger

Grigsons Ltd			SL 21
Details	£	Details	£
SDB – 10356	199.20	SRDB – CN668	72.00

We can now see that Grigsons Ltd owes the business £(199.20 – 72.00) = £127.20.

Task 2

(a) Complete the following sentences:

An invoice is entered on the	left	side of the customer's
	right	account
An credit note is entered on the	left	side of the customer's
	right	account

(b) The ledger account for Harris & Sons is shown here:

Harris & Sons			SL 17
Details	£	Details	£
SDB – 10358	120	SRDB – CN669	96

How much does Harris & Sons owe the business?

£ [ ]

ANALYSED SALES DAY BOOK

Most organisations include a more detailed analysis of net sales into different categories in their sales day books, by using analytical columns in an ANALYSED SALES DAY BOOK.

HOW IT WORKS

A business that makes sales of its products around the country may wish to analyse its sales by geographical area. Its analysed Sales Day Book might look something like this:

Date	Customer	Invoice number	Ref	Invoice total £	VAT £	Net £	North £	South £	East £	West £
1 June	AB Ltd	936	SL23	120.00	20.00	100.00		100.00		
1 June	CD & Co	937	SL03	240.00	40.00	200.00			200.00	
2 June	EF Ltd	938	SL45	64.80	10.80	54.00	54.00			
3 June	GH Ltd	939	SL18	144.00	24.00	120.00				120.00
4 June	IJ Bros	940	SL25	72.00	12.00	60.00		60.00		
				640.80	106.80	534.00	54.00	160.00	200.00	120.00

This type of Sales Day Book shows the net total from each invoice then breaks each one down into the separate geographical areas. Shading is often used to denote the analysis columns.

A business may also wish to analyse its sales by type of product. For example, a computer manufacturer may wish to analyse net sales between computers, printers and scanners. In this case there would be a column for each in the Sales Day Book. The Sales Returns Day Book should be analysed in the same manner.

Task 3

An extract from an invoice for a computer manufacturer that analyses its sales into those for computers, printers and scanners is given below:

Quantity	Description	£
1	GH3 Computer	800.00
1	Z3 Colour printer	300.00
1	S4 Scanner	200.00
		1,300.00
VAT		260.00
		1,560.00

Show how this invoice would be entered into the analysed Sales Day Book.

Invoice total £	VAT £	Net £	Computers £	Printers £	Scanners £

INVOICES AND THE ANALYSED PURCHASES DAY BOOK

Of course, a business that makes sales will also make purchases of goods and services. All of the invoices the business receives from its credit suppliers for a period are initially recorded by the business in a book of prime entry which is known as the PURCHASES DAY BOOK. (These invoices are, of course, recorded in the Sales Day Book of the supplier which is making the sale.) The Purchases Day Book is nearly always analysed into different types of purchases or expenses.

HOW IT WORKS

A typical analysed Purchases Day Book would look like this:

Supplier	Invoice number	Supplier code	Invoice total £	VAT £	Net £	Purchases £	Telephone £	Stationery £
Haley Ltd	33728	PL 25	60.00	10.00	50.00			50.00
JJ Bros	242G	PL 14	1,440.00	240.00	1,200.00	1,200.00		
B Tel	530624	PL 06	156.00	26.00	130.00		130.00	

BPP
LEARNING MEDIA

The writing up of the Purchases Day Book for a period has the following steps:

Step 1   Gather the invoices that have been received from suppliers since the day book was last written up. All the information needed to enter into the purchases day book is on the face of each invoice.

Step 2   Enter the date of the invoice, the name of the supplier and the supplier's invoice number in the appropriate columns – note that as all suppliers are likely to have different ways of numbering their invoices, the invoice numbers in the purchases day book will not be sequential.

Step 3   The supplier code column is entered with the account number for the supplier. The supplier code is the account number given to the supplier in the purchases ledger (which we will come back to shortly) and therefore is often given the prefix 'PL'. This code is important as it helps with the eventual entry of these figures into the accounts.

Step 4   Enter the figures from the invoice.

- The invoice total column contains the invoice total including VAT.

- The VAT is the amount shown on the face of the invoice.

- The net total on the invoice (ie the invoice total less the VAT) is then entered into the net total column and into appropriate analysis columns, which are often shaded in practice to denote their separation from the net total. This is where the Purchases Day Book differs from the Sales Day Book in that there are likely to be different types of invoice being received and therefore an analysed Purchases Day Book is nearly always used.

THE PURCHASES LEDGER

For each individual credit supplier the business needs to keep a record of how much it owes to that supplier at any one time. The way this is done is to record each invoice total in the supplier's ledger account in the PURCHASES LEDGER, a record that contains ledger accounts for every credit supplier. As we saw in Chapter 1, suppliers which the business owes money to are also known as TRADE PAYABLES.

Each credit supplier's ledger account contains two sides:

- On the **right-hand side** we record invoices, which **increase** the amount owed to the supplier

- On the **left-hand side** we record credit notes, settlement discounts and payments to the supplier, all of which **decrease** the amount owed to the supplier.

HOW IT WORKS

Step 1   Find the individual supplier's account in the purchases ledger using the supplier code.

Step 2   Enter the invoice total of the invoice, which is the amount the business actually owes to the supplier, on the right-hand side of this account.

Step 3   In the 'details' section next to the amount, enter 'PDB' followed by the invoice number (and the date if required).

Looking back at the three invoices entered in the Purchases Day Book, they would be entered in the purchases ledger as follows:

Purchases ledger

		Haley Ltd	PL 25
Details	£	Details	£
		PDB – 33728	60.00

		JJ Bros	PL 14
Details	£	Details	£
		PDB – 242G	1,440.00

		B Tel	PL 06
Details	£	Details	£
		PDB – 530624	156.00

The details for each entry is the supplier's invoice number recorded in the Purchases Day Book (PDB). The invoice number is entered as this will be useful when dealing with supplier enquiries.

CREDIT NOTES AND THE PURCHASES RETURNS DAY BOOK

Just as invoices received from suppliers are initially entered in their own book of prime entry, so too are credit notes – in the PURCHASES RETURNS DAY BOOK. This looks very similar to the Purchases Day Book with the same analysis columns and the same details needing to be entered.

HOW IT WORKS

A typical Purchases Returns Day Book would look like this:

Date 20XX	Supplier	Credit note number	Supplier code	Credit note total £	VAT £	Net £	Purchases £	Telephone £	Stationery £
4 May	Haley Ltd	CN783	PL25	24.00	4.00	20.00			20.00
5 May	JJ Bros	C52246	PL14	69.60	11.60	58.00	58.00		

The only difference here is that the credit note number is entered rather than an invoice number – and again these will not be sequentially numbered, as they are the suppliers' numbers. All of the details required can be found on the face of the credit note that is used to write up the Day Book.

Now we must enter each individual credit note in the supplier's account in the purchases ledger. The amount to be used is the **credit note total** and this must be entered in the **left-hand side** of the ledger account as it is a decrease in how much we owe the supplier.

Step 1   Find the individual supplier's account in the purchases ledger using the supplier code.

Step 2   Enter the credit note total, which is the amount of the reduction in what the business actually owes, on the left-hand side of this account.

Step 3   In the 'details' section next to the amount, enter '**PRDB**' followed by the **credit note number** (and the date if required).

Purchases ledger

		Haley Ltd		PL 25
Details	£	Details		£
PRDB – CN783	24.00	PDB – 33728		60.00

Task 4

(a)   Complete the following sentences:

An invoice is entered on the	left	side of the supplier's account
	right	
A credit note is entered on the	left	side of the supplier's account
	right	

(b)   With reference to the ledger account above, the business owes Haley Ltd

£ [   ]

Task 5

An extract from an invoice from a supplier of dishwashers is given below:

Quantity	Description	£
1	RDX dishwasher	650.00
1	KJG dishwasher	480.00
1	XXX dishwasher	520.00
		1,650.00
VAT		330.00
		1,980.00

Show how this invoice would be entered into the analysed Purchases Day Book for a business that retails dishwashers and other electrical goods to consumers.

Invoice total £	VAT £	Net £	Purchases £	Expenses £

THE CASH BOOK FOR RECEIPTS

For receipt of money into the business's bank account and for payments from it, the book of prime entry is known as the CASH BOOK. We shall look first at the cash book in relation to receipts.

All money being paid into the bank account is recorded in the cash book whether it is payments by cash, cheque, credit card, debit card or directly through the banking system by automated payment.

The types of receipt that an organisation has depends entirely on the nature of its business. However for most businesses the following are typical:

- Cash sales
- Money received from trade receivables for credit sales
- Money paid into the business by the owner
- Bank interest paid by the bank
- Miscellaneous income such as rent, commission income and proceeds of sales of assets held for a long time, such as a car

Most businesses will have an ANALYSED CASH BOOK which reflects the most common types of receipt.

HOW IT WORKS

A typical Cash Book for receipts is shown below, though you should note that in practice a variety of formats are possible:

Date	Details	Ref	Bank £	VAT £	Discount allowed £	Cash sales £	Sales ledger £	Sundry £
10 May	Grigsons Ltd	SL21	127.20				127.20	

Date – the date recorded will be the date the payment was received or written up in the cash book, depending upon the organisation's policy.

Details – the details should be sufficient to describe the transaction so that it can easily be analysed and checked at a later date, eg if a receipt from a trade receivable, the name of that trade receivable.

Ref – the reference will depend upon the type of receipt. If it is a receipt from a trade receivable then the reference will normally be the customer code from the sales ledger for that trade receivable.

Bank – the figure in the 'Bank' column is the total amount of the receipt paid into the business's bank account.

VAT – when money is received from a trade receivable no VAT is recorded, as the VAT was recorded when the original sales invoice was entered into the Sales Day Book. However, when cash sales which include VAT are made, the VAT element must be entered in this column, and the sale element must be entered into the 'cash sales' column (see below), so that the total of the two amounts is the figure in the Bank column.

Discount allowed – the DISCOUNT ALLOWED column is known as a 'memorandum column', which is why it is shaded here. What is recorded here is the amount of any settlement discount that has been deducted by a credit customer before making the payment.

Cash sales – the net amount of the cash sale, the total banked minus the VAT, is recorded in this column. Remember that when we refer to a cash sale we mean a sale that is not on credit – the actual receipt could be in the form of cash, cheque, credit or debit card.

Sales ledger – this column is used to record the amount of receipts from credit customers (trade receivables). The details of VAT, net total and invoice total were recorded in the Sales Day Book when the sales invoice was sent out to the customer. When the customer pays the invoice only the total of the actual payment needs to be recorded here. The amount is the actual value of the payment received, that is after deduction of any settlement discount that was offered.

Sundry – the sundry column is used for other miscellaneous receipts that do not occur on a regular basis, such as payments into the business by its owner, interest paid by the bank, rental income and income received on commission. It is important that their 'details' and reference coding are detailed enough for the receipt to be identified.

Task 6

Identify whether the following statement is True or False.

VAT can only be recorded in the Cash Book for receipts that have not come from credit customers.

True	
False	

Finally, we enter each receipt into the customer's account in the sales ledger. The amount to be used is the amount in the 'Bank' column and this must be entered in the **right-hand side** of the ledger account as it is a **decrease** in how much the customer owes us.

Step 1   Find the individual customer's account in the sales ledger using the customer code.

Step 2   Enter the amount from the Bank column, which is the amount of the reduction in what the customer actually owes, on the right-hand side of this account.

Step 3   In the 'details' section next to the amount, enter '**CB**' (this can be followed by another code number such as the number of the customer's remittance advice if this is available). Enter the date if this is required.

Sales ledger

Grigsons Ltd			SL 21
Details	£	Details	£
SDB – 10356	199.20	SRDB – CN668	72.00
		CB	127.20

Task 7

With reference to the ledger account above, Grigsons Ltd owes the business:

£ [   ]

THE CASH BOOK FOR PAYMENTS

When payments are made by a business out of its bank account for any purpose, like receipts they are initially recorded in the CASH BOOK. The cash book for payments is the mirror image of the cash book for receipts.

All money being paid out of the bank account is recorded in the cash book whether it is payment by cheque, banker's draft (a type of cheque which cannot be cancelled), debit card or directly through the banking system by automated payment.

Automated payments are usually authorised by the business, such as to pay employees or suppliers by BACS or CHAPS, or to pay regular bills by standing order or direct debit. Sometimes it is the bank itself that authorises the payment, as when it deducts interest that the business owes to the bank.

There is normally an ANALYSED CASH BOOK for payments as there will be different reasons for making the payment.

HOW IT WORKS

The layout of a typical analysed Cash Book for payments is shown below:

Date	Details	Ref	Bank £	VAT £	Discounts received £	Cash purchases £	Purchases ledger £	Petty cash £	Sundry £
10 May	Haley Ltd	PL 25	36.00				36.00		

Date – the date will be the date on which the transaction was authorised (such as when the cheque was written or the BACS payment was notified to the bank) or the date on which the cash book is written up, depending upon the organisation's policy.

Details – the details should be sufficient to describe the payment so that it can be easily analysed and checked at a later date – the usual details to enter will be a cheque or BACS reference number and the name of the person being paid.

Ref – the reference will depend upon the type of payment that is being made. If the payment is to a credit supplier (trade payable) then the reference will be the supplier code (the purchases ledger account number for the supplier).

Bank – the figure in the bank column is the total value of the payment leaving the bank account.

VAT – when a payment is made to a trade payable no VAT is recorded, as the VAT was recorded and posted to the VAT account when the original purchase invoice was entered into the Purchases Day Book. However, if other types of payment are made on which VAT is charged – ie cash purchases – the VAT element is recorded in the VAT column, so that the total of the two amounts is the figure in the Bank column.

Discounts received – like the discount allowed column in relation to receipts, the DISCOUNTS RECEIVED column is known as a 'memorandum' column, which is why it is shaded here. What is recorded is the amount of any settlement discount that was deducted by the business before the payment was made to the supplier. This column will be used when the payment is recorded in the purchases ledger.

Cash purchases – if the payment is for purchases of goods that are not bought on credit, the net amount of the purchase is entered in this column. This is often calculated as the total amount of the payment less that VAT element. Remember that a cash purchase is one that does not involve a period of credit – the actual purchase will be by cheque or debit card rather than with cash.

Purchases ledger – this column is used to record the payments made to credit suppliers. The details of VAT, net total and invoice total were recorded in the purchases day book when the invoice was received from the supplier. When the supplier is paid only the total amount of the actual payment need be recorded here, after the deduction of any settlement discount that is taken.

Petty cash – this column is used to record any amounts that are taken out of the bank account in the form of notes and coins to be placed in the petty cash box.

Sundry – this column is used for the net amount of any other payments that are made from the bank account, such as for interest payable to the bank.

Task 8

When should VAT be recorded in the Cash Book in relation to payments? Tick one.

On all payments

On any payments that are not payments to credit suppliers (trade payables)

Finally, we enter each payment in the supplier's account in the purchases ledger. The amount to be used is the amount in the 'Purchases ledger' column and this must be entered in the **left-hand side** of the ledger account as it is a **decrease** in how much the business owes the supplier.

Step 1   Find the individual supplier's account in the purchases ledger using the supplier code.

Step 2   Enter the amount from the purchases ledger column, which is the amount of the reduction in the amount owed to the supplier, on the left-hand side of this account.

Step 3   In the 'details' section next to the amount, enter '**CB**' (this can be followed by another code number such as the number of the cheque if this is appropriate). Enter the date if this is required.

Purchases ledger

	Haley Ltd		**PL 25**
Details	£	Details	£
PRDB – CN783	24.00	PDB – 33728	60.00
CB	36.00		

Task 9

With reference to the ledger account above, the business owes Haley Ltd:

£ [   ]

THE PETTY CASH BOOK FOR PAYMENTS

As we saw in Chapter 1, most businesses keep a small amount of notes and coin, known as PETTY CASH, on hand to meet the need to:

- Make small purchases of items such as stamps, stationery and milk

- Reimburse employees for small amounts of expenditure that they have made on the business's behalf

When a payment out of its petty cash is made by a business, for any purpose, a petty cash voucher (like the one we saw in Chapter 1) is prepared and initially recorded as a payment in the ANALYSED PETTY CASH BOOK. This book of prime entry is very similar to the analysed cash book for payments, as there will be different types of payment made by an organisation.

HOW IT WORKS

The layout of a typical analysed Petty Cash Book for payments is shown below:

Date	Details	Voucher number	Total cash £	VAT £	Postage £	Stationery £	Other £
10 May	Stationery – Lara Moschetta	067	48.00	8.00		40.00	
10 May	Post office – stamps	068	15.00		15.00		
10 May	Green Clean – window cleaning	069	30.00				30.00

Date – the date will be the date on which the cash was paid out and the petty cash voucher was written or the date on which the petty cash book is written up, depending upon the organisation's policy.

Details – the details should be sufficient to describe the payment so that it can be easily analysed and checked at a later date – the usual details to enter will be the type of expenditure (stationery), and the name of the person being paid, eg Lara Moschetta.

Voucher number – this is the petty cash voucher number, since payments can only be made if a petty cash voucher has been prepared.

Total cash – this is the total amount of the payment leaving the petty cash box.

VAT – when a payment is made to a supplier such as a shop, or to an employee in reimbursement for something that they have paid for, there may be an amount of VAT included in the payment. The VAT element is recorded separately in the VAT column.

Travel, postage, stationery, other – if the payment is for purchases and expenses that are not bought on credit, the net amount (amount net of VAT) is entered in one of these columns.

THE PETTY CASH BOOK FOR RECEIPTS

For receipts of cash into the business's petty cash box the book of prime entry is also the PETTY CASH BOOK, this time for receipts. The only receipt that you are likely to encounter is of cash that has been taken out of the bank account specifically to be held as petty cash.

HOW IT WORKS

A typical Petty Cash Book for receipts is shown below:

Date	Details	Total £
10 May	Cash	200.00

Date – the date recorded will be the date the cash was received or written up in the petty cash book, depending upon the organisation's policy.

Details – the details should be sufficient to describe the transaction so that it can easily be analysed and checked at a later date.

Total – the figure in the 'Total' column is the total amount of the receipt paid into the business's petty cash box.

CHAPTER OVERVIEW

- In order to reduce the number of entries necessary in the ledger accounts, documents of the same type are initially recorded in the books of prime entry

- Sales invoices are all recorded initially in the Sales Day Book (SDB), which shows the net amount, VAT and invoice totals from each invoice; the net amount may also be analysed to show the different types of sale

- The invoice total from each individual sales invoice must also be entered into the individual trade receivable's account in the sales ledger

- Sales credit notes are initially recorded in the Sales Returns Day Book (SRDB). It shows the net amount, VAT and credit note total from each credit note, and may be analysed. The credit note total is also entered in the individual trade receivable's account in the sales ledger

- Purchases invoices are all recorded initially in the Purchases Day Book (PDB). It shows the net amount, VAT and invoice totals from each invoice, and the net amount is nearly always analysed to show the different types of purchase or expense

- The invoice total from each individual purchase invoice must also be entered into the individual trade payable's account in the purchases ledger

- Purchases credit notes from suppliers are initially recorded in the Purchases Returns Day Book (PRDB). It shows the net amount, VAT and credit note total from each credit note, and may be analysed. The credit note total is also entered in the individual trade payable's account in the purchases ledger

- Receipts into the business's bank account are recorded in the Cash Book (CB)

- Receipts from credit customers are entered from the Cash Book into the customer's account in the sales ledger

- Payments from the business's bank account are recorded in the Cash Book

- Payments to credit suppliers are entered from the Cash Book into the supplier's account in the purchases ledger

- Payments from petty cash, normally for small business purchases, are recorded in the Petty Cash Book (PCB). Receipts of petty cash, normally taken from the bank account, are also recorded in the Petty Cash Book

Keywords

Books of prime entry – the books in which the details of the organisation's transactions are initially recorded prior to entry into the ledger accounts

Day books – another name for books of prime entry

Sales Day Book (SDB) – primary record for recording sales invoices in credit sales

Ledger account – the record of all the transactions made by the business with a credit customer

Sales ledger – record that contains ledger accounts for every credit customer

Trade receivables – credit customers who owe money to the business

Sales Returns Day Book (SRDB) – the primary record for recording credit notes sent to credit customers

Analysed Sales Day Book – a Sales Day Book where the net figure is analysed into the different types of sale for each invoice

Purchases Day Book (PDB) – primary record for recording purchases invoices in credit purchases

Purchases ledger – record that contains ledger accounts for every credit supplier

Trade payables – credit suppliers to whom the business owes money

Purchases Returns Day Book (PRDB) – the primary record for recording credit notes received from credit suppliers

Cash Book (CB) – the book of prime entry in which all **receipts** into and **payments** from the business's bank account are recorded

Analysed Cash Book – a cash book which reflects the most common types of receipt

Discount allowed – column of CB which records settlement discounts deducted by credit customers

BACS – Bankers Automated Clearing Service – automated payment method

CHAPS – Clearing House Automated Payment System – electronic transfer of money between two bank accounts

Discounts received – column of CB which records amount of any settlement discounted deducted by the business before the payment was made to the supplier

Petty Cash – small amounts of cash held on the premises to cover day-to-day expenses

Petty Cash Book – the book of prime entry for recording payments out of and receipts into petty cash

TEST YOUR LEARNING

Test 1

Write up the Sales Day Book and the Sales Returns Day Book from the invoices and credit notes given below.

Sales Day Book

Date	Customer	Invoice number	Customer code	Invoice total £	VAT £	Net £
Total						

Sales Returns Day Book

Date	Customer	Credit note number	Customer code	Credit note total £	VAT £	Net £
Total						

Invoice no. 44263	1 June	J Jepson	SL34	£118.00 + VAT
Invoice no. 44264	2 June	S Beck & Sons	SL01	£320.00 + VAT
Credit note 3813	2 June	Scroll Ltd	SL16	£18.00 + VAT
Invoice no. 44265	3 June	Penfold Ltd	SL23	£164.00 + VAT
Invoice no. 44266	4 June	S Beck & Sons	SL01	£256.00 + VAT
Invoice no. 44267	4 June	J Jepson	SL34	£144.00 + VAT
Credit note 3814	5 June	Penfold Ltd	SL23	£16.80 + VAT

Test 2

Today's date is 6 June and you are required to write up the Purchases Day Book and the Purchases Returns Day Book from the invoices and credit notes given below. It is organisational policy to use the date column to record the date of entry rather than the date of invoice.

Purchases Day Book

Date	Supplier	Invoice number	Supplier code	Invoice total £	VAT £	Net £
Total						

Purchases Returns Day Book

Date	Supplier	Credit note number	Supplier code	Credit note total £	VAT £	Net £
Total						

1 June	Invoice 224363 from Y H Hill (PL16)	£158.40 + VAT
1 June	Credit note CN92 from Letra Ltd (PL24)	£100.00 + VAT
2 June	Invoice PT445 from Letra Ltd (PL24)	£228.00 + VAT
2 June	Invoice 77352 from Coldstores Ltd (PL03)	£158.00 + VAT
5 June	Credit note C7325 from Y H Hill (PL16)	£26.00 + VAT

Test 3

Write up the Cash Book from the details of receipts and payments given below.

Cash Book – receipts

Date	Details	Ref	Bank £	VAT £	Disc allowed £	Cash sales £	Sales ledger £	Sundry £

Cash Book – payments

Date	Details	Ref	Bank £	VAT £	Disc received £	Cash purchases £	Purchases ledger £	Petty cash £	Sundry £

Receipt	1 June	J Jepson	SL34	£220.00, discount £10
Payment	2 June	Letra Ltd	PL24	£500.00, discount £20
Payment	2 June	Cash purchase		£48.00 including VAT
Receipt	3 June	Cash sale		£72.00 including VAT

chapter 4:
ACCOUNTING FOR CREDIT SALES

---

chapter coverage 📖

This chapter considers in more detail all of the documents involved in making credit sales, and the checks that must be made on those documents. We recap the recording of invoices and credit notes in the books of prime entry and we cover the preparation of statements of account for customers, before going on to the checking of payments received from credit customers. The topics covered are:

✍ The documents involved in credit sales

✍ The checks that must be made when preparing a sales invoice

✍ The procedure for preparing credit notes

✍ The procedures for authorisation and coding of sales invoices and credit notes

✍ The documents involved and the checks to be made when receiving payments from customers

✍ The procedure for preparing statements of accounts for customers

DOCUMENTS INVOLVED IN CREDIT SALES

The diagram below gives an overview of the main documents potentially involved in a credit sale from initial customer enquiry to final settlement of the invoice. We have already looked at some of these documents when we recorded them in the day books, but in this chapter our aim is to examine in more detail the sequence of processes involved in accounting for credit sales.

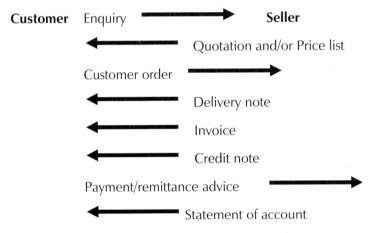

Quotation and price list

The credit sale process will normally be initiated by the customer making an enquiry about the purchase of goods. The seller replies to the customer's enquiry confirming that the requested goods can be supplied, on what date and at what price. This may be done verbally, or by sending a PRICE LIST and/or a QUOTATION.

HOW IT WORKS

Earlier today, Southfield Electrical's sales department received a phone call from the purchasing manager of Whitehill Superstores enquiring whether Southfield could supply six Zanpoint dishwashers as soon as possible. Southfield is able to supply these so the sales department sends out the following quotation and extract from its price list.

QUOTATION

Southfield Electrical
Industrial Estate
Benham DR6 2FF
Tel 0303379 Fax 0303152
VAT Reg 0264 2274 49

To:

Whitehill Superstores
28, Whitehill Park
Benham DR6 5LM

Date: 3 Sept 20XX

Number: 04217

Thank you for your enquiry of earlier today. We are pleased to confirm that we can deliver the following goods on the day after receiving your purchase order.

6 Zanpoint dishwashers (Code 4425) at a price of £200 each, excluding VAT.

Authorised: *I Hampton*

Sales Manager

SOUTHFIELD ELECTRICAL		
PRICE LIST (extract)		
Product code	**Product description**	**Unit price (excl VAT) £**
Zanpoint 4425	Dishwasher	200.00

Customer order

The purchasing manager at Whitehill has received this quotation and price list and finds the price and terms acceptable. The purchasing department will produce the order shown next, which as far as Southfield is concerned is a CUSTOMER ORDER.

ORDER

WHITEHILL SUPERSTORES
28 Whitehill Park
Benham DR6 5LM
Tel 0303446 Fax 0303447

To: Southfield Electrical
Industrial Estate
Benham
DR6 2FF

Number: 32011

Date: 5 Sept 20XX

Delivery address: Whitehill Superstores
28, Whitehill Park
Benham DR6 5LM

Product code	Quantity	Description	Unit list price £
4425	6	Zanpoint Dishwasher	200 (excluding VAT)

Authorised by: *P. Winterbottom* **Date:** *5 Sept 20XX*

Let's consider the details of this order:

- Using a coding system it has its own unique, sequential document number which will be quoted on subsequent documentation such as the delivery note and invoice

- The address to which the goods are to be delivered is given, as this may be different from the address of the purchasing department if there is, for example, a separate warehouse

- The product is described in words but is also given a product code – coding is useful in all areas of the accounting process to identify goods and transactions. If a code is used as well as words it helps to reduce the chances of an error being made in the sale, but it is very important that the code is used accurately in every detail

- The price has been confirmed in order to avoid any misunderstanding at a later date

- The order must be signed and authorised by an appropriate person within Whitehill Superstores

Task 1

Who issues an order?

The buyer of goods	
The seller of goods	

Delivery note

Once the order is received by the sales department of Southfield Electrical it will be checked against the quotation number 04217 to ensure that this was the quantity and price that had been quoted to Whitehill. The delivery of the goods must then be organised. The sales department will draw up the DELIVERY NOTE, shown next, to accompany the dishwashers.

DELIVERY NOTE

Southfield Electrical
Industrial Estate
Benham DR6 2FF
Tel 0303379 Fax 0303152

Delivery address:

Whitehill Superstores
28, Whitehill Park
Benham DR6 5LM

Number: 34619
Date: 6 Sept 20XX
Order number: 32011

Product code	Quantity	Description
4425	6	Zanpoint Dishwasher

Received by: [Signature] .... **Print name:** ....

Date: ....

On the delivery note:

- The address of the delivery is included so that the carrier knows where to take the goods.

- The delivery note has its own unique, sequential number which can be used on other documentation and in any dispute.

- The order number relating to this delivery is also included in order to be able to match the delivery note to the order easily.

- A precise description of the goods is given both by including the description in words and including the product code. Again, this is important as the goods despatched must be exactly what the customer has ordered.

- When the delivery note leaves Southfield it is unsigned. The signature that is required is that of the person receiving the dishwashers at Whitehill. The stores department at Whitehill must check that the goods that have been delivered were the ones ordered and stated on the delivery note. If there is any discrepancy then this must be recorded on the delivery note.

- There will normally be more than one copy of the delivery note. Once it has been signed to confirm that the correct goods have been delivered, the carrier and the customer will keep one copy each as proof of delivery and a further copy will be returned to Southfield as proof of delivery and acceptance by Whitehill.

- No price information is included on the delivery note as this is not relevant at this stage.

Invoice

The next stage in the process is for Southfield Electrical to produce a sales INVOICE. This is the request for payment for the dishwashers from Whitehill Superstores and details precisely how much is due and when.

INVOICE	Invoice number 56314
Southfield Electrical **Industrial Estate** **Benham DR6 2FF** **Tel: 01239 345639**	
VAT registration:	0264 2274 49
Date/tax point:	7 September 20XX
Order number:	32011
Customer:	Whitehill Superstores 28 Whitehill Park Benham DR6 5LM
Account number (customer code)	SL 44

Description/product code	Quantity	Unit amount £	Total £
Zanpoint dishwashers /4425	6	200.00	1,200.00
Net total			1,200.00
VAT at 20%			240.00
Invoice total			1,440.00
Terms 30 days net			

The invoice is prepared by the sales department with reference to the information on the order (its number is included on the invoice to help the customer trace the details), quotation/price list and delivery note. We shall see more about preparing invoices later in this chapter.

Writing up the Sales Day Book and sales ledger

As we saw in Chapter 3, this invoice must be entered by Southfield into its Sales Day Book and from there into the sales ledger account for Whitehill (note that in this sales ledger account, some other entries have already been made, and we have used dates here as we shall shortly be preparing a statement of account, but note that in your assessment you may not need to insert dates).

Sales Day Book

Date 20XX	Customer	Invoice number	Customer code	Total £	VAT £	Net £
7 Sept	Whitehill	56314	SL44	1,440.00	240.00	1,200.00

Sales ledger

Whitehill Superstores   SL 44

Date	Details	£	Date	Details	£
21/8	SDB – 56019	316.40	28/8	SRDB – 08613	47.46
7/9	SDB – 56314	1,440.00			

Credit note

If a damaged dishwasher is returned to Southfield then notification is needed. A RETURNS NOTE may be sent by Whitehill to Southfield with details, or alternatively, Southfield may raise its own returns note when the goods are received back. Southfield's stores department must ensure that the dishwasher is in fact returned damaged, then Southfield will issue a CREDIT NOTE to Whitehill which reverses the part of the sales invoice that relates to the damaged dishwasher.

CREDIT NOTE	Credit note number 08641		
Southfield Electrical **Industrial Estate** **Benham DR6 2FF** **Tel: 01239 345639**			
VAT registration:	0264 2274 49		
Date/tax point:	12 September 20XX		
Order number:	32011		
Customer:	Whitehill Superstores 28 Whitehill Park Benham DR6 5LM		
Account number (customer code)	SL 44		
Description/product code	Quantity	Unit amount £	Total £
Zanpoint dishwasher /4425 Reason for credit note: Delivered damaged	1	200.00	200.00
Net total			200.00
VAT at 20%			40.00
Credit note total			240.00
Terms 30 days net			

The credit note is prepared by Southfield with reference to the information on the order (its number is included on the credit note to help the customer trace the details), quotation/price list and returns note. The calculations are done by the sales department.

The credit note is entered by Southfield into its Sales Returns Day Book and from there into the sales ledger account for Whitehill.

Sales Returns Day Book

Date 20XX	Customer	Credit note number	Customer code	Total £	VAT £	Net £
12 Sept	Whitehill	08641	SL44	240.00	40.00	200.00

Sales ledger

	Whitehill Superstores				SL 44
Date	Details	£	Date	Details	£
21/8	SDB – 56019	316.40	28/8	SRDB – 08613	47.46
7/9	SDB – 56314	1,440.00	12/9	SRDB – 08641	240.00

Receipt from a customer

At some stage the credit customer will pay the supplier for goods that have been supplied. This may be by cheque, debit or credit card payment or by automated payment from the customer's bank account to the supplier's.

HOW IT WORKS

Suppose that on 20 September Whitehill Superstores paid Southfield Electrical by cheque the amount that it owed to the company at the beginning of September, which was for invoice 56019 received on 21 August for £316.40 less credit note number 08613 for £47.46 received on 28 August. Along with the cheque it sends the supplier the following remittance advice note, which we saw first in Chapter 1.

REMITTANCE ADVICE NOTE	Remittance advice note number
Whitehill Superstores 28 Whitehill Park Benham DR6 5LM	0937498
Supplier:	**Southfield Electrical** **Industrial Estate** **Benham DR6 2FF**
Account number (supplier code)	**PL 526**

Date	Transaction reference	Amount £
21/08/XX	Invoice 56019	316.40
28/08/XX	Credit note 08613	(47.46)
20/09/XX	Payment made – cheque enclosed	268.94

The receipt is entered by Southfield into its Cash Book and from there into the sales ledger account for Whitehill.

Cash Book

Date	Details	Ref	Bank £	VAT £	Discount allowed £	Cash sales £	Sales ledger £	Sundry £
20 Sept	Whitehill Superstores	SL44	268.94				268.94	

Sales ledger

Whitehill Superstores **SL 44**

Date Details	£	Date Details	£
21/8 SDB – 56019	316.40	28/8 SRDB – 08613	47.46
07/9 SDB – 56314	1,440.00	12/9 SRDB – 08641	240.00
		20/9 CB	268.94

Statements of account for credit customers

There is one final document in the document cycle for credit sales and that is the STATEMENT OF ACCOUNT. This shows all the invoices and credit notes that have been sent to the customer that month together with any amounts outstanding from previous months, along with any payments received from the customer in the month. It is common practice to send out statements to

customers on a regular basis, usually monthly. The customer can use the statement to check that its records are complete. Often it is following receipt of a statement that discrepancies between the records of customers and suppliers come to light.

Southfield Electrical's statement of account to Whitehill Superstores might look like this:

STATEMENT OF ACCOUNT				
Southfield Electrical				
Industrial Estate				
Benham DR6 2FF				
Tel: 01239 345639				
VAT registration:		0264 2274 49		
Date:		30 September 20XX		
Customer:		Whitehill Superstores 28 Whitehill Park Benham DR6 5LM		
Account number (customer code)		SL 44		
Date	Details	Debit £	Credit £	Balance £
21.08.XX	Inv56019	316.40		316.40
28.08.XX	CN08613		47.46	268.94
07.09.XX	Inv56314	1,440.00		1,708.94
12.09.XX	CN08641		240.00	1,468.94
20.09.XX	Payment received – thank you		268.94	1,200.00
Amount now due				1,200.00

HOW IT WORKS

Let's now consider how to prepare this statement from Whitehill Superstores' sales ledger account:

- Address it to Whitehill Superstores and again, in order to ease finding the relevant information, include the customer code

- Prepare it in date order, so the transactions in the sales ledger account are entered in chronological order, starting with the 21 August invoice

- The credit note of 28 August is shown along with the invoice on 7 September and the credit note sent out on 12 September (at this stage do not worry about the terms debit and credit or which column each entry goes into: this will become clear later in the Text)

- The payment received on 20 September in respect of the invoice on 21 August and the credit note on 28 August is shown last, by convention with the narrative 'Payment received – thank you'

- After each entry the amount currently owing by Whitehill – the BALANCE – is shown

- By the end of September the amount due is the September invoice less the September credit note, £1,440.00 – £240.00 = £1,200.00

The next time a statement is prepared the August invoice and credit note and the September payment will not be shown, as the latter 'clears' the former.

Often customers will return payments with a copy of their statement on which the items that are being paid are ticked off. Alternatively, the statement sent out by the seller may include a tear-off REMITTANCE ADVICE NOTE at the bottom which allows the customer to show which invoices from the statement are being paid. The customer will then return the remittance advice note to the supplier together with the payment.

A typical combined statement and remittance advice is shown on the next page.

STATEMENT OF ACCOUNT				
Southfield Electrical **Industrial Estate** **Benham DR6 2FF** **Tel: 01239 345639**				
VAT registration:	0264 2274 49			
Date:	31 October 20XX			
Customer:	Whitehill Superstores 28 Whitehill Park Benham DR6 5LM			
Account number (customer code)	SL 44			

Date	Details	Debit £	Credit £	Balance £
01.10.XX	Balance from Sept	1,200.00		1,200.00
02.10.XX	Inv56389	2,448.45		3,648.45
15.10.XX	Inv56436	1,118.23		4,766.68
18.19.XX	CN08662		123.80	4,642.88
28.10.XX	Payment received – thank you		1,200.00	3,442.88
Amount now due				3,442.88

REMITTANCE ADVICE			
To: Southfield Electrical **Industrial Estate** **Benham DR6 2FF**	From: Whitehill Superstores 28 Whitehill Park Benham DR6 5LM		
Account number (customer code)	SL 44		
Please indicate the items you are paying ✓ and return with your payment			
Details	**Debit** **£**	**Credit** **£**	✓
Inv56389 Inv56436 CN08662	2,448.45 1,118.23	 123.80	
Payment enclosed **£**			

PREPARING AND CHECKING INVOICES

There are a lot of details and calculations involved in preparing an invoice and it is extremely important that these details and calculations are done properly and thoroughly checked.

We will now work through the whole process of preparing a sales invoice in order to illustrate all of the checks that must be made.

HOW IT WORKS

You work for Southfield Electrical and are responsible for preparing sales invoices. Today is 8 October 20XX and you have on your desk the following customer order from Whitehill Superstores for which an invoice must be prepared.

ORDER

WHITEHILL SUPERSTORES
28 Whitehill Park
Benham DR6 5LM
Tel 0303446 Fax 0303447

To: Southfield Electrical
Industrial Estate
Benham
DR6 2FF

Number: 32174

Date: 2 Oct 20XX

Delivery address: Whitehill Superstores
28, Whitehill Park
Benham DR6 5LM

Product code	Quantity	Description	Unit list price £
6160	4	Hosch Washing Machine	300.00
3172	10	Temax Mixer	40.00

Authorised by: *P. Winterbottom* **Date:** *2 Oct 20XX*

Step 1   You must first check that the goods were in fact sent to Whitehill and therefore you find the delivery note that relates to order 32174. This is given below.

DELIVERY NOTE

Southfield Electrical
Industrial Estate
Benham DR6 2FF
Tel 0303379 Fax 0303152

Delivery address:

Whitehill Superstores
28, Whitehill Park
Benham DR6 5LM

Number: 34772

Date: 5 Oct 20XX

Order number: 32174

Product code	Quantity	Description
6160	4	Hosch Washing Machine
3172	9	Temax Mixer

Received by: [Signature] *J. Jones*   **Print name:** *J. JONES*

Date: *5 Oct 20XX*

Step 2   You should note that only nine mixers were delivered and accepted (the delivery note is signed by J Jones at Whitehill) and therefore only nine mixers must be invoiced, not the ten that were ordered. You might also make a note to follow up why only nine and not ten were delivered, or to inform the appropriate person in your organisation.

Step 3   The prices quoted on the order are the unit list prices. You must now check that these list prices are correct. An extract from Southfield's price list is given below.

SOUTHFIELD ELECTRICAL

PRICE LIST (extract)

Product code	Product description	Unit price (excl VAT) £
HOSCH		
6040	Tumble dryer	250.00
6050	Tumble dryer	280.00
6060	Tumble dryer	300.00
6140	Washing machine	220.00
6150	Washing machine	260.00
6160	Washing machine	300.00
6170	Washing machine	340.00
TEMAX		
3160	Food processor	100.00
3162	Food processor	120.00
3164	Food processor	140.00
3170	Mixer	35.00
3172	Mixer	40.00
3174	Mixer	46.00

The prices included on the order agree with the list prices and therefore can be used on the invoice.

Step 4 You must now find the customer file for Whitehill Superstores which will show details of addresses, customer codes and DISCOUNT POLICY in respect of the customer (ie what trade, bulk and settlement discounts should be applied to sales to the customer).

The customer file for Whitehill Superstores shows the following:

- Customer code – SL44

- Discount policy effective 1 Oct 20XX:

  – 10% trade discount is allowed

  – 5% bulk discount on orders where list price net of trade discount exceeds £1,000

  – 4% settlement discount for payment within 10 days, otherwise net 30 days

Step 5 You now have all of the information required to start preparing the invoice. The final invoice is now shown and we will then work through the remaining steps in completing it.

INVOICE	Invoice number 56483		
Southfield Electrical Industrial Estate Benham DR6 2FF Tel: 01239 345639			
VAT registration:	0264 2274 49		
Date/tax point:	8 October 20XX		
Order number:	32174		
Customer:	Whitehill Superstores 28 Whitehill Park Benham DR6 5LM		
Account number (customer code)	SL 44		
Description/product code	Quantity	Unit amount £	Total £
Hosch washing machine /6160	4	300.00	1,200.00
Temax Mixer /3172	9	40.00	360.00
List price			1,560.00
Less: trade discount 10%			(156.00)
List price net of trade discount			1,404.00
Less: bulk discount 5%			(70.20)
Net total			1,333.80
VAT at 20%			256.09
Invoice total			1,589.89
Terms			
4% discount for settlement within 10 days of invoice date, otherwise 30 days net			

Step 6 Enter the customer's name and address and customer code from the customer file. The invoice number is the next number in sequence after the previous invoice. Enter today's date.

Step 7   Enter the quantities, codes and descriptions from the delivery note – remember that only nine mixers were delivered.

Step 8   Enter the unit prices from the price list. Calculate the total list price by multiplying the quantity by the list price:

$$4 \times £300 \quad = \quad £1,200.00$$

$$9 \times £40 \quad = \quad £360.00$$

Step 9   Calculate the total list price by adding together the totals for each product:

$$£1,200.00 + £360.00 = £1,560.00$$

Step 10 Calculate the trade discount as 10% of the total list price:

$$£1,560.00 \times 10\% \ (10/100) = £156.00$$

Deduct the trade discount:

$$£1,560.00 - £156.00 = £1,404.00$$

Step 11 As the list price less trade discount is more than £1,000, calculate the bulk discount as 5% of the list price net of trade discount:

$$£1,404.00 \times 5\% \ (5/100) = £70.20$$

Deduct the bulk discount to arrive at the net total:

$$£1,404.00 - £70.20 = £1,333.80$$

Step 12 To calculate the VAT, first of all determine the amount of settlement discount (round it down):

$$£1,333.80 \times 4\% \ (4/100) = £53.35$$

In a working deduct this from the net total:

$$£1,333.80 - £53.35 = £1,280.45$$

Calculate the VAT at 20% based on the amount after the discount has been deducted:

$$£1,280.45 \times 20\% \ (20/100) = £256.09$$

Step 13 Add the VAT calculated to the net total to arrive at the (gross) invoice total:

$$£1,333.80 + £256.09 = £1,589.89$$

Step 14 Enter the settlement discount terms at the bottom of the invoice.

BPP
LEARNING MEDIA

PREPARING CREDIT NOTES

When preparing a credit note the same types of procedure need to be followed as those for an invoice. The approach as listed below should be followed:

- Check that the goods were actually returned by reference to the returns note

- Ensure that the credit note is being issued to the correct customer

- Check that the goods returned are the ones on the credit note by checking the product code

- Check the price of the returned goods on the price list and/or quotation

- Check the calculations on the credit note, eg quantity × unit price = total price

- Check that any trade and bulk discounts that applied to the invoice have been allowed for in relation to the goods returned

- Check that the VAT has been correctly calculated, remembering to adjust for a settlement discount if this adjustment had been made on the original invoice

CODING AND AUTHORISING INVOICES AND CREDIT NOTES

Coding invoices and credit notes

Invoices and credit notes must be coded for their eventual inclusion in the accounting records using the business's coding system. The invoice or credit note should always include the customer code (also known as the sales ledger or account code); with Whitehill Superstores this was SL 44. There may also be a coding to indicate what type of sale was made, or the geographical region of the sale. If this is the policy of the organisation then each invoice must be correctly coded to show the type of product or where the sale was made.

HOW IT WORKS

Southfield Electrical is considering a coding system which allows it to code sales according to the type of sale made. It has revised its price list to show sales codes as follows:

SOUTHFIELD ELECTRICAL			
PRICE LIST (extract)			
Product code	Sales code	Product description	Unit price (excl VAT) £
HOSCH			
6040	H6	Tumble dryer	250.00
6050	H6	Tumble dryer	280.00
6060	H6	Tumble dryer	300.00
6140	H6	Washing machine	220.00
6150	H6	Washing machine	260.00
6160	H6	Washing machine	300.00
6170	H6	Washing machine	340.00
TEMAX			
3160	T3	Food processor	100.00
3162	T3	Food processor	120.00
3164	T3	Food processor	140.00
3170	T3	Mixer	35.00
3172	T3	Mixer	40.00
3174	T3	Mixer	46.00

A sales invoice using the sales codes would look like this:

INVOICE	Invoice number 56484
Southfield Electrical **Industrial Estate** **Benham DR6 2FF** **Tel: 01239 345639**	
VAT registration:	0264 2274 49
Date/tax point:	8 October 20XX
Order number:	56237
Customer:	Rampton Ltd 45 Janes Trading Estate Benham DR6 8DF
Account number (customer code)	SL 62

Description/product code	Quantity	Unit amount £	Total £	Sales code
Hosch tumble dryer /6040	2	250.00	500.00	<u>H6</u>
Temax food processor /3162	4	120.00	<u>480.00</u>	<u>T3</u>

Net total	980.00
VAT at 20%	196.00
Invoice total	1,176.00
Terms 30 days net	

In the analysed Sales Day Book the sale can now be analysed using the sales codes.

Sales Day Book

Date 20XX	Customer	Invoice number	Customer code	Total £	VAT £	Net £	H6 £	T3 £
8 Oct	Rampton	56484	SL62	1,176.00	196.00	980.00	500.00	480.00

Authorisation of invoices and credit notes

An invoice is a very important document for a business. It is the source of the business's income and therefore the invoice must be accurate. As such, once the invoice has been prepared it will be checked and once the checking process has taken place will be marked as checked. This might be with a simple signature or with a standardised rubber stamp showing exactly what checks have been carried out, eg calculations, price lists, customer codes etc.

The precise checks and method of indicating that those checks have been carried out will differ from organisation to organisation. However the final outcome will be that the invoice will be authorised by the appropriate person in the organisation and then sent out to the customer. There should be checks in place to ensure that an invoice that has not been authorised cannot be sent out to a customer. This also applies to credit notes.

PAYMENTS FROM CUSTOMERS

The next stage of the credit sale process is for the customer to pay the business. This may be by:

- Cheque through the post
- Automated payment from the customer's bank account to the supplier's
- Debit or credit card payment over the phone or on the internet
- Cash (occasionally – we shall not consider this method further here)

In each case the business must check to ensure that the amount of the receipt:

- Is accurately calculated

- Is valid, ie it ties in with supporting documentation (the remittance advice note, statement of account, invoice and sales ledger account)

Once these checks have been completed the receipt will be recorded in the Cash Book.

Remittance advice note

When a payment is received the first check that must be carried out is that it is for the correct amount. In order to do this you will need to know what invoices are being paid. In many situations a REMITTANCE ADVICE NOTE will be received with the payment detailing precisely what the payment relates to.

The remittance advice may have been prepared by the customer or it may be a blank remittance advice sent out by your organisation either with the regular statements that are sent to customers or with the invoice itself.

Here is a typical remittance advice:

REMITTANCE ADVICE

To: Southfield Electrical
Industrial Estate
Benham
DR6 2FF
Tel 0303379 Fax 0303152

From: Dagwell Enterprises
Number: 012561
Account no: PL 813
Date: 22 September 20XX

Reference	Amount	Paid (✔)
30112	723.80	✔
30126	811.59	✔
CN2351	218.65	✔
30164	928.83	
CN2377	239.70	

CHEQUE ENCLOSED	£1,316.74

You must check that the total of the invoices and credit note indicated as being paid does agree to the payment amount (£723.80 + £811.59 – £218.65 = £1,316.74).

If the customer has prepared the remittance advice by completing the invoice and credit note amounts then you should also check that correct amounts have been included. This can be done by examining the sales ledger account for that customer in the sales ledger.

Valid cheques

When payment is received in the form of a cheque then you must ensure that the cheque itself is valid. We shall come back to this in Basic Accounting II.

Correct settlement discount

If the customer has taken advantage of a settlement discount then very careful checks must be made to ensure that this discount is both valid and correctly calculated.

- Has this customer been offered a settlement discount? This can be checked either by examining the copy of the invoice or finding the discount policy in relation to this customer which will include details of the settlement discount that is routinely offered to this customer.

- Has the invoice been paid within the timescale set for the settlement discount? For this the copy of the invoice should be examined to determine the invoice date and the terms of the settlement discount. For example if an invoice was dated 10 September and a settlement discount was offered for payment received within ten days, if the payment was received before or on 20 September it would be valid, but if payment arrived after this date then the claiming of the discount would not be valid.

- Has the discount been correctly calculated? Again, the invoice will need to be checked for this as, due to the VAT complication with settlement discounts, the discount has to be calculated as a percentage of the VAT exclusive amount and the VAT then added on.

HOW IT WORKS

An extract from a sales invoice shows the following:

	£
Net total	600.00
VAT	115.20
Invoice total	715.20
Terms 4% settlement discount for payment received within 10 days of invoice, otherwise net 30 days	

The discount that can be deducted is 4% of the net total £600.00

$£600.00 \times 4/100 = £24.00$

Therefore the payment that is received should be for £715.20 – £24.00 = £691.20.

Payment received without a remittance advice note

If a customer sends a payment without a remittance advice note and it is in settlement of more than one invoice, you must examine the customer's account in the sales ledger to determine which invoices are being paid by this payment.

HOW IT WORKS

Southfield Electrical has received this cheque through the post with no accompanying documentation.

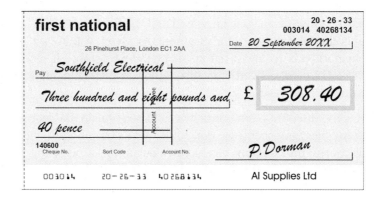

Clearly, this cheque is from A1 Supplies Ltd and therefore the account for this customer should be found in the sales ledger. The customer's account shows the following:

	A1 Supplies Ltd				SL 41
Date	Details	£	Date	Details	£
3 Sept	SDB – 30118	115.68	12 Sept	SDB – CN2355	35.97
8 Sept	SDB – 30131	228.69			
15 Sept	SDB – 30144	147.25			
19 Sept	SDB – 30159	279.46			

By trial and error you find that the following invoices less the credit note add up to the cheque total:

	£
30118	115.68
30131	228.69
CN 2355	(35.97)
	308.40

PROCEDURE FOR CHECKING PAYMENTS FROM CUSTOMERS

Cheques and remittance advices

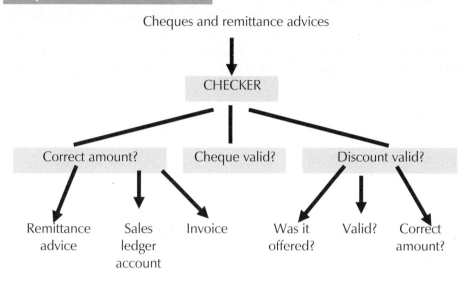

Task 2

Goods with a net total of £400.00 were sold to a customer and VAT of £76.00 was added to the net total to give a gross invoice total of £476.00. The invoice was dated 20 November and a cheque for £456.00 was received today, 28 November. The invoice terms stated that a 5% settlement discount was offered for payment received within 14 days of the invoice date.

Is the receipt for the correct amount?

Yes

No

Automated payments

Many customers pay amounts due by automated payment, such as by Bankers Automated Clearing System (BACS) or online transfer, from their bank accounts into the supplier's. This means that your organisation's bank account will be credited directly with the amount of the payment. Normally the customer will send your organisation notification that the payment is being made in the form of a remittance advice note showing precisely which invoices are being paid.

The same checks should be carried out as for a receipt of a cheque:

- Has the correct amount been transferred?
- If a settlement discount has been taken, is this valid and correct?

If no remittance advice or other notification is sent by the customer, the credit to your organisation's bank account will be noticed when the cash book and the bank statement sent by the bank itself are compared on a regular basis. When the credit is spotted, it will be necessary to work out which invoices have been paid by this automated payment, as we saw above with any other payment not accompanied by a remittance advice note.

Errors in payments

In this chapter we have considered a number of checks that must be made on payments received (or receipts):

- Is the payment for the correct amount, or has the customer overpaid or underpaid?

- Is the payment valid?

- Has the settlement discount been correctly calculated and should it have been taken?

Any discrepancy in the amount is usually caused by:

- The customer underpaying an invoice by mistake, for instance by making a payment of £210.36 when the invoice was for £210.63, so the customer still owes 27p

- The customer overpaying the invoice by mistake, for instance by making a payment of £54.00 when the invoice was for £45.00, so the business owes the customer £9.00

- The customer deducting the wrong amount of settlement discount, for instance by calculating it on the invoice total rather than the net total

- The customer deducting settlement discount even though the deadline for taking advantage of this is past

Where there is a discrepancy the following actions must be taken:

- Record the payment as received in the Cash Book

- Report the discrepancy to the appropriate person within the organisation. In most cases the customer will need to be informed of the problem and may possibly be asked to issue a replacement cheque or make an additional automated payment.

CHAPTER OVERVIEW

- When credit sales are made there are potentially many documents involved

- The process is started by an initial enquiry from the prospective customer

- The seller then answers the enquiry with a quotation and/or a price list

- The customer confirms with an order

- The goods are despatched to the customer with a delivery note that must be signed by the customer upon receipt of the goods and a copy returned to the seller

- The seller sends out an invoice requesting payment from the customer

- Upon return of any goods from the customer, the seller will send out a credit note effectively cancelling all or part of the invoice

- A statement of account is sent out to the customer on a regular basis, normally monthly, showing invoices and credit notes issued during the month, payments received (if any) and the final amount outstanding from the customer at the end of the month

- Many checks are necessary when preparing an invoice to ensure that it is for the correct goods, to the correct customer and for the correct amount

- Similar checks are also required for credit notes, in particular details of the goods that have been returned

- Each organisation will have its own procedures that should be followed for authorisation and coding of sales invoices and credit notes

- Organisations that make credit sales will receive most payments from customers in the form of automated transfers into their bank account or cheques through the post

- The receipt must be thoroughly checked – is it for the correct amount? – is the payment valid? – is any settlement discount deducted valid and correctly calculated?

- If no remittance advice is received with the payment then the customer's sales ledger account must be examined to determine which invoices (less credit notes) are being paid

- If any discrepancies arise with a payment from a customer the payment should still be recorded, but the discrepancy should be reported to the appropriate person within the organisation

Keywords

Price list – written confirmation from a supplier as to the price of goods

Quotation – a written statement sent from supplier to customer advising them of the price of a specific good or service (or combination of the two)

Customer order – sent from the customer to the seller confirming the required purchase

Delivery note – document sent to the customer with the items being despatched which must be signed by the customer confirming receipt of the items

Invoice – a document that clearly sets out what money is owed by a named trade receivable to a named trade payable in respect of particular goods or services

Returns note – the document sent by the purchaser to the seller detailing the goods returned and the reason for their return

Credit note – a document stating that a certain amount has been credited to the buyer's account

Statement of account – a statement sent out to credit customers on a regular basis showing the amount outstanding and due from the customer at the end of the period

Remittance advice note – a document setting out exactly how a payment is made up (ie the invoices/credit notes that it is paying/netting off)

Discount policy – a company's system for giving discounts to customers in order to encourage certain buying behaviours

TEST YOUR LEARNING

Test 1

Using the picklist below, identify which type of document would be used for the following purposes.

To inform the customer of the amount due for a sale	
To inform the seller of the quantities required	
To inform the seller that some of the delivery was not of the standard or type required	
To inform the customer of the quantity delivered	
To inform the customer that the invoiced amount was overstated	

Picklist:

Delivery note
Returns note
Quotation
Invoice
Credit note
Customer purchase order

Test 2

(a) A customer is purchasing 23 items each with a list price of £56.00. A trade discount of 15% is given to this customer.

Calculate the total cost before the discount, the discount, the net of discount price, the VAT and the total cost.

	£
Cost before discount	
Trade discount	
Net of discount price	
VAT	
Total cost	

(b) Suppose that a settlement discount of 3% is also offered. Calculate the same figures on this basis.

	£
Cost before discount	
Trade discount	
Net of discount price	
VAT	
Total cost	

Test 3

Given below is a sales invoice. Check it carefully, state what is wrong with it and calculate the correct figures.

INVOICE

Southfield Electrical
Industrial Estate
Benham DR6 2FF
Tel 0303379 Fax 0303152
VAT Reg 0264 2274 49

To: G. Bender & Sons
14, High St.
Wentford
DR10 6LT

Invoice number: 56503

Date/tax point:

Order number: 32216

Account number:

Quantity	Description	Stock code	Unit amount £	Total £
21	Zanpoint Tumble Dryer	4610	180.00	3,870.00
10	Temax Mixer	3172	40.00	400.00
				4,270.00
Less:	15% discount			683.20

Net total	3,586.80
VAT	717.36
Invoice total	4,304.16

Terms
5% cash discount for payment within 10 days, otherwise 30 days net
E & OE

Errors:

Corrected figures

	£
Tumble dryers	
Mixers	
Goods total	
Trade discount	
Net total	
VAT	
Invoice total	

Test 4

Given below are four sales invoices for Southfield Electrical.

(a)   Write up the Sales Day Book using these invoices

(b)   Total the columns of the Sales Day Book

Date	Customer	Invoice number	Customer code	Invoice total £	VAT £	Net £
	Totals					

INVOICE

Southfield Electrical
Industrial Estate
Benham DR6 2FF
Tel 0303379 Fax 0303152
VAT Reg 0264 2274 49

To: Dagwell Enterprises
Dagwell House
Hopchurch Rd
Winnish
DR2 6LT

Invoice number: 56401

Date/tax point: 21 Sept 20XX

Order number: 6123

Account number: SL 15

Quantity	Description	Product code	Unit amount £	Total £
3	Milo Dishwasher	8641	310.00	930.00
Less:	15% discount			139.50

Net total		790.50
VAT		158.10
Invoice total		948.60

Terms
Net 30 days
E & OE

4: Accounting for credit sales

INVOICE

Southfield Electrical
Industrial Estate
Benham DR6 2FF
Tel 0303379 Fax 0303152
VAT Reg 0264 2274 49

To:
G. Thomas & Co
48, High Street
Cabland
DR3 8QT

Invoice number: 56402

Date/tax point: 21 Sept 20XX

Order number: 6124

Account number: SL 30

Quantity	Description	Product code	Unit amount £	Total £
16	Zanpoint Tumble Dryer	3462	220.00	3,520.00
11	Temax Kettle	6180	15.00	165.00
				3,685.00
Less:	20% discount			737.00

Net total	2,948.00
VAT	566.01
Invoice total	3,514.01

Terms
4% discount for settlement within 10 days of invoice date, otherwise net 30 days
E & OE

BPP
LEARNING MEDIA

INVOICE

Southfield Electrical
Industrial Estate
Benham DR6 2FF
Tel 0303379 Fax 0303152
VAT Reg 0264 2274 49

To:

Polygon Stores
Grobler Street
Parrish
DR7 4TT

Invoice number: 56403

Date/tax point: 22 Sept 20XX

Order number: 6127

Account number: SL 03

Quantity	Description	Product code	Unit amount £	Total £
4	Milo Dishwasher	8641	310.00	1,240.00
2	Milo Washing Machine	8649	290.00	580.00
				1,820.00
Less:	10% discount			182.00

Net total	1,638.00
VAT	327.60
Invoice total	1,965.60

Terms
Net 30 days
E & OE

INVOICE

Southfield Electrical
Industrial Estate
Benham DR6 2FF
Tel 0303379 Fax 0303152
VAT Reg 0264 2274 49

To:
Weller Enterprises
Booker House
Industrial Estate
Benham
DR6 2FM

Invoice number: 56404

Date/tax point: 23 Sept 20XX

Order number: 6128

Account number: SL 18

Quantity	Description	Product code	Unit amount £	Total £
2	Habark cooker	1264	480.00	960.00

Net total	960.00
VAT	184.32
Invoice total	1,144.32

Terms
4% discount for settlement within 10 days of invoice date, otherwise net 30 days
E & OE

Test 5

Here are two cheques received by Southfield Electrical in the post this morning and the accompanying remittance advices. Check that the correct amount has been sent in each case. Today's date is 22 October 20XX.

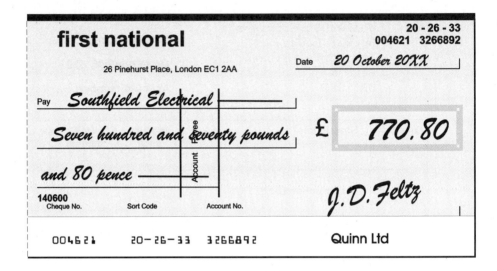

REMITTANCE ADVICE

To: Southfield Electrical
Industrial Estate
Benham
DR6 2FF
Tel 0303379 Fax 0303152

From: Quinn Ltd

Date: 20 October 20XX

Reference	Amount	Paid (✓)
30128	325.61	✓
CN2269	18.80	✓
30201	463.27	✓

CHEQUE ENCLOSED	£770.08

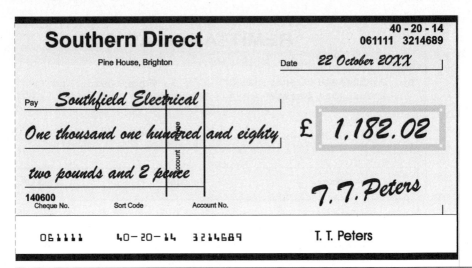

REMITTANCE ADVICE

To: Southfield Electrical
Industrial Estate
Benham
DR6 2FF
Tel 0303379 Fax 0303152

From: T.T. Peters

Date: 22 October 20XX

Reference	Amount	Paid (✓)
30196	556.28	✓
30217	180.53	✓
30223	267.03	
30237	454.21	✓

CHEQUE ENCLOSED	£1,182.02

Test 6

Southfield Electrical have received a cheque from a customer, Long Bros, for £226.79 with no accompanying documentation. The sales ledger account for this customer is given below. Determine which invoices/credit notes are being paid by this cheque.

Long Bros			SL 42
Details	£	Details	£
SDB – 30219	88.37	SRDB - CN2381	15.80
SDB – 30234	157.35		
SDB – 30239	85.24		
SDB – 30250	265.49		

Invoice/credit note number	£
Total	

Test 7

The following transactions all took place on 30 November and have been entered into the Sales Day Book as shown below. No entries have yet been made into the ledger system.

Sales Day Book

Date 20XX	Details	Invoice number	Total £	VAT @ 20% £	Net £
30 Nov	Fries & Co	23907	2,136	356	1,780
30 Nov	Hussey Enterprises	23908	3,108	518	2,590
30 Nov	Todd Trading	23909	3,720	620	3,100
30 Nov	Milford Ltd	23910	2,592	432	2,160
	Totals		11,556	1,926	9,630

What will be the entries in the sales ledger?

Sales ledger

Account name	Amount £	Left side of account ✓	Right side of account ✓	Details in account

Test 8

Sales invoices have been prepared and partially entered in the analysed Sales Day Book, as shown below.

(a) Complete the entries in the Sales Day Book by inserting the appropriate figures for each invoice.

(b) Total the last five columns of the Sales Day Book.

Sales Day Book

Date 20XX	Details	Invoice number	Total £	VAT @ 20% £	Net £	Sales type 1 £	Sales type 2 £
30 Nov	Wright & Co	5627		2,000		10,000	
30 Nov	H Topping	5628	1,560				1,300
30 Nov	Sage Ltd	5629	600			500	
	Totals						

Test 9

On 1 December Wendlehurst Trading delivered the following goods to a credit customer, Stroll In Stores.

Wendlehurst Trading

Delivery note No. 8973
01 Dec 20XX

Stroll In Stores   Customer account code:
ST725

600 1 litre bottles Tiger pop, product code TIG300.

The list price of the goods was £10 per case of 12 bottles plus VAT. Stroll In Stores are to be given a 15% trade discount and a 4% early settlement discount.

Complete the invoice below.

Wendlehurst Trading
VAT Registration No. 876983479

Stroll In Stores   Customer account code:
                                                     Delivery note number:

                                                     Date: 1 Dec 20XX

Invoice No: 624

Quantity of cases	Product code	Total list price £	Net amount after discount £	VAT £	Gross £

Test 10

The following is a summary of transactions between Wendlehurst Trading and Holroyda, a new credit customer.

£4,390 re invoice 5607 of 18 November
£1,400 re invoice 5612 of 21 November
£160 re credit note 524 of 22 November
£980 re invoice 5616 of 29 November
Payment of £4,000 received 30 November

Complete the statement of account below.

Wendlehurst Trading VAT Registration No. 876983479			
To: Holroyda			Date: 30 Nov 20XX
Date 20XX	Details	Transaction amount £	Outstanding amount £

chapter 5:
ACCOUNTING FOR CREDIT PURCHASES

ORDERING GOODS

We have seen how the business document cycle works when looking at it from the viewpoint of the seller of goods. Now we will look at it in more detail from the purchaser's side.

The initial stage is that of ordering the goods. This can be done in a variety of ways:

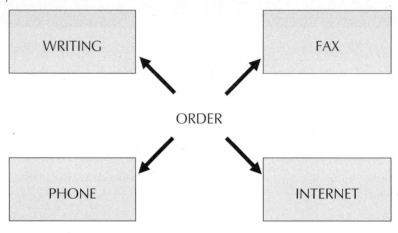

In writing or by fax

Perhaps still the most common way of ordering goods is in writing. This could be in the form of a letter but if many orders are placed with suppliers then it is more likely that the organisation will have pre-printed and sequentially numbered purchase order forms.

The order seen in Chapter 4 that was a customer order from the point of view of the seller (Southfield Electrical) is a PURCHASE ORDER from the point of view of the buyer (Whitehill Superstores).

PURCHASE ORDER

WHITEHILL SUPERSTORES
28 Whitehill Park
Benham DR6 5LM
Tel 0303446 Fax 0303447

To: Southfield Electrical
Industrial Estate
Benham
DR6 2FF

Number: 32011

Date: 5 Sept 20XX

Delivery address: Whitehill Superstores
28, Whitehill Park
Benham DR6 5LM

Product code	Quantity	Description	Unit list price £
4425	6	Zanpoint Dishwasher	200 (excluding VAT)

Authorised by: *P. Winterbottom*   **Date:** *5 Sept 20XX*

The purchase order is from Whitehill Superstores to Southfield Electrical and details the quantity, the specific item and the agreed price. The important issue from Whitehill's side is that it is properly authorised. Obviously, it is necessary for any business to ensure that only goods that are absolutely necessary are purchased, and therefore there should be strict controls over who can authorise purchase orders.

Over the phone

Goods are often ordered by phone, particularly where either the buyer and seller are well known to each other or the purchases are of small quantities. If an order is placed over the phone the most important issue is that a record is kept of what has been agreed in case of future dispute. The buyer may ask the seller for a confirmation of the order that has been placed or, at the very least, make a file note of the price and any other terms agreed over the phone.

On the internet

Goods can be ordered over the internet if it is an allowed method of ordering items according to the organisation's policy manual, and if it has been authorised by an appropriate member of senior staff. Many internet orders are actually cash purchases using the business debit card, but in this chapter we shall assume that they are all credit transactions.

When placing an order, ensure that a copy is printed out to be placed on file.

Order details

Whatever method of ordering is used, a copy of the order details must be kept in the filing system in the accounts department. This will be compared with the seller's delivery note and invoice to ensure that only goods that have been properly authorised for ordering are received and paid for.

RECEIVING GOODS

Once the goods have been ordered, the next stage in the process is that they will be received. This will usually take place in the stores department or warehouse and an important part of the process takes place here.

When the goods arrive they will normally be accompanied by a delivery note. The DELIVERY NOTE used in Chapter 4 for the delivery from Southfield to Whitehill is reproduced below:

DELIVERY NOTE

Southfield Electrical
Industrial Estate
Benham DR6 2FF
Tel 0303379 Fax 0303152

Delivery address:

Whitehill Superstores
28, Whitehill Park
Benham DR6 5LM

Number: 34619
Date: 6 Sept 20XX
Order number: 32011

Product code	Quantity	Description
4425	6	Zanpoint Dishwasher

Received by: [Signature] *R. Stansted*   **Print name:** *R. STANSTED*

Date: *6 Sept 20XX*

- The delivery note details the quantity and precise description of the goods using both the description in words and the product code

- There is no price as this is not relevant in the stores department

- The delivery note includes the related order number

- The delivery note must be signed to evidence the fact that these goods have been delivered

The signature of the stores personnel is extremely important. It proves that the carrier of the goods did indeed deliver these goods and that the purchaser actually received them.

The most important point for the stores personnel to check is that the quantity actually delivered is what is stated on the delivery note. In some cases, it may be possible to check that none of the goods have any defects at the time of delivery but normally this will take place later. The initial signature from the stores manager on this delivery note is simply evidence that this number of these precise goods were delivered on this date.

Goods received note

In many organisations, in addition to signing the delivery note, an internal document will also be filled out by the stores department known as the GOODS RECEIVED NOTE. This is completed once there has been an opportunity to examine the goods in more detail. A goods received note for the delivery to Whitehill from Southfield is shown below:

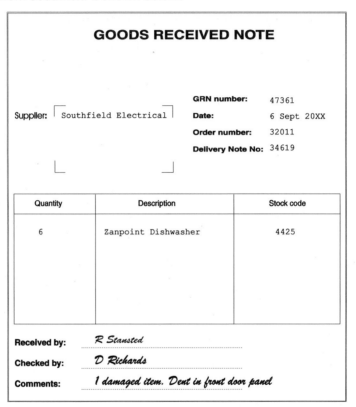

Note the main points:

- The goods received note (GRN) has its own sequential number

- It is referenced to the order number and delivery note number, both taken from the copy of the supplier's delivery note kept by the stores department

- The quantity and precise detail of the goods received are noted

- In order to ensure the security of the goods being received, the GRN is not only signed by the person who received delivery of the goods but also by a second person who checked them

- Once there has been a chance to examine the goods in detail, any comments on their condition can then be added to the GRN. Note that in this case one of the machines is damaged and this has been noted.

Documentation for the accounts department

Once the stores department has dealt with checking the goods, all the documentation is then passed over to the accounts department. At this stage the accounts department potentially has a price list and quotation from the seller, a purchase order, a delivery note and a goods received note.

The accounts department must check that the delivery note agrees with the purchase order to ensure that what was ordered has actually arrived. The details should then be compared with the goods received note to ensure that the goods that were actually delivered were of the correct quality and condition.

RETURNING GOODS

If the goods supplied are the wrong ones or are not of the quality or in the condition expected they will be returned to the seller. Often the return of the goods will be accompanied by a RETURNS NOTE detailing the goods returned and the reason for their return. The contents of this are very similar to the goods received note.

Whitehill Superstores	**RETURNS NOTE**	
Supplier	Southfield Electrical	
Goods received note number		47361
Returns note number		8909
Date		7 Sept 20XX
Order number		32011
Delivery note number		34619
Quantity	**Description**	**Product code**
1	Zanpoint dishwasher	4425
Returned by	D Richards	
Comment	Dent to front door panel	

CHECKING THE INVOICE AND CREDIT NOTE

The next item in the purchase cycle is the receipt of the INVOICE from the seller. This is the document that will eventually form the authorisation for payment of the amount due to the seller. Many checks must be carried out on this invoice before it is authorised for payment.

Step 1   Have the goods been received? Agree the details to the purchase order, the delivery note and the goods received note. Do they all agree in terms of quantity, quality and price? In the scenario of Whitehill and Southfield the following invoice is received from Southfield:

INVOICE	Invoice number 56314		
Southfield Electrical **Industrial Estate** **Benham DR6 2FF** **Tel: 01239 345639**			
VAT registration:	0264 2274 49		
Date/tax point:	7 September 20XX		
Order number:	32011		
Customer:	Whitehill Superstores 28 Whitehill Park Benham DR6 5LM		
Account number (customer code)	SL 44		
Description/product code	**Quantity**	**Unit amount £**	**Total £**
Zanpoint dishwashers /4425	6	200.00	1,200.00
Net total			1,200.00
VAT at 20%			240.00
Invoice total			1,440.00
Terms 30 days net			

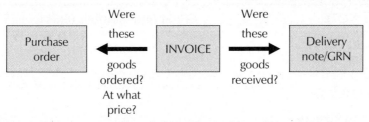

This invoice is for the six dishwashers delivered although only five were of acceptable quality. The delivery note shows that six dishwashers were delivered but the goods received note indicates that one was not of acceptable quality.

The accounts department would check that a returns note was sent when the damaged dishwasher was returned and would not pay the invoice until the related credit note was received.

When the CREDIT NOTE arrives it is again checked to the file of documentation on this purchase which now consists of (potentially):

- Quotation and price list
- Purchase order
- Delivery note
- Goods received note
- Returns note
- Invoice

CREDIT NOTE	Credit note number 08641
Southfield Electrical **Industrial Estate** **Benham DR6 2FF** **Tel: 01239 345639**	
VAT registration:	0264 2274 49
Date/tax point:	12 September 20XX
Order number:	32011
Customer:	Whitehill Superstores 28 Whitehill Park Benham DR6 5LM
Account number (customer code)	SL 44

Description/product code	Quantity	Unit amount £	Total £
Zanpoint dishwasher /4425 Reason for credit note: Delivered damaged	1	200.00	200.00
Net total			200.00
VAT at 20%			40.00
Credit note total			240.00
Terms 30 days net			

Step 2   Are the calculations on the documents correct?

HOW IT WORKS

The invoice and credit note considered so far have been very uncomplicated. However, when trade, bulk and settlement discounts are introduced the checks that have to be made become more involved.

Given below is the more complex invoice that Whitehill Superstores received from Southfield Electrical in Chapter 4:

INVOICE	Invoice number 56483		
Southfield Electricals **Industrial Estate** **Benham DR6 2FF** **Tel: 01239 345639**			
VAT registration:	0264 2274 49		
Date/tax point:	8 October 20XX		
Order number:	32174		
Customer:	Whitehill Superstores 28 Whitehill Park Benham DR6 5LM		
Account number (customer code)	SL 44		
Description/product code	**Quantity**	**Unit amount** **£**	**Total** **£**
Hosch washing machine /6160	4	300.00	1,200.00
Temax Mixer /3172	9	40.00	<u>360.00</u>
List price			1,560.00
Less: trade discount 10%			<u>(156.00)</u>
List price net of trade discount			1,404.00
Less: bulk discount 5%			(70.20)
Net total			1,333.80
VAT at 20%			256.09
Invoice total			1,589.89
Terms 4% discount for settlement within 10 days of invoice date, otherwise 30 days net			

Task 1

The net total of goods purchased from a supplier is £1,600 and the supplier has offered a settlement discount of 5%. What is the correct amount of VAT to be charged on the invoice?

£

The checks that should be made on this invoice are as follows. The same sorts of checks will apply to credit notes:

- Compare the purchase order, delivery note and goods received note to the invoice to ensure that the correct quantity has been invoiced

- Check the percentage discounts agree to the discount policy agreed with this supplier: 10% trade discount, 5% bulk discount for orders over £1,000, 4% settlement discount for payment within ten days

- Check that the unit prices are correct – this may be noted from the seller's quotation or price list

- Check that the total price for each item has been correctly calculated by multiplying the unit price by the quantity, eg 4 × £300 = £1,200

- Check that the total list price has been correctly added up, eg £1,200 + £360.00 = £1,560.00

- Check that the trade discount has been correctly calculated, eg £1,560 × 10/100 = £156, and that it has been deducted correctly, eg £1,560.00 – £156.00 = £1,404.00

- Check that the bulk discount has been deducted as due (since the total after trade discount exceeds £1,000) and that it has been calculated correctly, eg £1,404.00 × 5/100 = £70.20; net total is therefore £1,404.00 – £70.20 = £1,333.80

- Check that the VAT is correct – remember that when a settlement discount is offered the VAT is calculated on the basis that the discount is actually taken:

	£
Net total	1,333.80
Less: settlement discount (£1,333.80 × 4/100)	(53.35)
	1,280.45
VAT £1,280.45 × 20/100.00	256.09

- Check that the VAT has been correctly added to the net total, eg £1,333.80 + £256.09 = £1,589.89

Services received

One of the initial checks on goods is that they are actually received, evidenced by a delivery note or goods received note. With services there will not be any physical goods.

It is still important to check that the services that have been invoiced have been received. Typical invoices for services might include utilities such as electricity, gas and phone bills. Such bills can usually be checked to meter readings and for reasonableness, for example each organisation should have an idea of the normal value of the phone bill and therefore if a very different amount is billed then this should be investigated.

Other services that may be invoiced are items such as cleaning services carried out by contractors. There should be evidence of the hours that have been worked and billed, such as clock cards or time sheets. Alternatively, service providers such as the cleaning contractors or annual auditors may have already agreed a fee, so the documentation for that agreement should be checked upon receipt of the invoice.

AUTHORISATION OF PURCHASE INVOICES

When the accuracy of an invoice has been thoroughly checked it is ready for payment at the appropriate time and is passed to the person in the accounts department who is responsible for making payments.

There must be some evidence to show that the invoice has been checked and is therefore correct and authorised for payment. Each organisation will have different methods of indicating that an invoice has been checked and authorised as illustrated below.

- The simplest method is for the invoice to be stamped or marked "pay" and signed by the checker

- A more detailed method might be to stamp the invoice with a standard checklist or attach such a checklist to the invoice to be marked off as each check is carried out, an example of which follows.

INVOICE AUTHORISATION		
	Initials	**Date**
Checked to order		
Checked to delivery note/GRN		
Unit price checked		
Trade/bulk discounts checked		
Total price checked		
VAT checked		
Authorised by:	**Date:**	

Settlement discounts

Some authorisation stamps may also include space for the amount of any settlement discount that can be deducted when making the payment. This should be calculated when checking the invoice and entered in this space.

The discount that can be deducted is the relevant percentage of the net total of goods, as the VAT calculation should have already taken the settlement discount into account.

An extract from an invoice where a 3% settlement discount has been offered is given:

	£
Net total of goods	2,000.00
VAT	388.00
Invoice total	2,388.00

The amount of settlement discount that could be deducted from the invoice total is 3% of the net total calculated as follows:

£2,000 × 3/100 = £60.00

This amount can be entered onto the authorisation stamp and the payer can decide whether or not to pay the invoice in time to claim the settlement discount. Alternatively, it may be the policy of the organisation that the discount is not calculated until the person responsible for paying the invoice deals with it.

Task 2

An invoice for goods shows the net total of the goods as £800.00 and the VAT as £155.20 giving a gross invoice total of £955.20. A settlement discount of 3% is offered. How much discount can be deducted?

£

Coding of purchase invoices/credit notes

The authorisation stamp or sheet may also have space for entries to be made to code the purchase invoice and/or credit note. The document will eventually have to be entered into the accounting records and the codes that may be included on the authorisation stamp would be:

- The supplier code, probably the purchase ledger account number

- A product code for the type of goods or service that is being invoiced in order to aid recording in the accounting records, especially in the analysed purchases day book where, as we saw in relation to the sales day book, analysis may be based on the prefixes of the product codes

WRITING UP THE PURCHASES DAY BOOK AND LEDGER

The invoice is entered by Whitehill Superstores into its Purchases Day Book and from there into the purchases ledger account for Southfield Electricals (the supplier code and purchases ledger account code are both PL 73).

Purchases Day Book

Date 20XX	Supplier	Invoice number	Supplier code	Total £	VAT £	Net £
8 Oct	Southfield Electricals	56483	PL 73	1,589.89	256.09	1,333.80

Purchases ledger

Southfield Electricals		PL 73	
Details	£	Details	£
		PDB – 56483	1,589.89

Where a credit note from a supplier has been received, the Purchases Returns Day Book and purchases ledger are written up.

RECONCILING SUPPLIERS' STATEMENTS

The final document that may be received by a buyer of goods from the seller is a statement of account. As we have already seen from the seller's side, this is produced by the seller on a regular basis and sent out to the buyer.

A supplier's statement of account is a very important double check on the accuracy of the buying organisation's accounting records. The statement is checked for accuracy to the individual supplier's account in the buyer's purchases ledger, with any differences carefully explained. This process is called RECONCILING supplier statements.

HOW IT WORKS

At the end of February 20XX Whitehill Superstores has the following transactions recorded in its purchases ledger account for Southfield Electricals:

Purchases Ledger

Southfield Electricals			PL 73
Details	£	Details	£
PRDB – CN09543	734.25	PDB – 58256	2,089.76
CB – auto payment	1,301.31	PDB – 58311	1,240.00
CB – discount taken	54.20	PDB – 58325	3,287.09

Whitehill Superstores knows that the history of the account in February is as follows:

- Three invoices from Southfield were recorded towards the end of the month.

- In respect of the first invoice (total £2,089.76) a credit note for £734.25 was received.

- Whitehill wished to settle the remaining amount of the first invoice (£2,089.76 – £734.25 = £1,355.51), after deducting a settlement discount of £54.20, so it sent a payment of £1,355.51 – £54.20 = £1,301.31.

- Whitehill has decided to leave paying the second two invoices until March, so at the end of February it owed Southfield £1,240.00 + £3,287.09 = £4,527.09.

Right at the beginning of March Whitehill receives the following statement of account from Southfield:

STATEMENT OF ACCOUNT	
Southfield Electricals **Industrial Estate** **Benham DR6 2FF** **Tel: 01239 345639**	
VAT registration:	0264 2274 49
Date:	28 February 20XX
Customer:	Whitehill Superstores 28 Whitehill Park Benham DR6 5LM
Account number (customer code)	SL 44

Date	Details	Amount £	Balance £
23 Feb	Invoice 58256	2,089.76	2,089.76
27 Feb	Credit note 09543	(734.25)	1,355.51
27 Feb	Invoice 58311	1,240.00	2,595.51
28 Feb	Invoice 58325	3,287.09	5,882.60
Amount now due			5,882.60
Terms 4% discount for settlement within 10 days of invoice date, otherwise 30 days net			

Evidently the customer and the supplier do not agree how much is outstanding. The difference between them is:

	£
Amount per supplier statement	5,882.60
Amount per purchases ledger	4,527.09
Difference	1,355.51

The supplier, Southfield Electricals, is saying that the customer, Whitehill Superstores, owes £1,355.51 more than Whitehill thinks it does.

By looking at the amount of the difference it is clear that Southfield Electricals thinks that Whitehill still owes the net amount of the first invoice and the credit note, while Whitehill shows in the purchases ledger account that it has settled this amount. This is confirmed when we note that the supplier's statement does not contain details of the automated payment made and settlement discount taken. Clearly, the automated payment had not yet reached Southfield Electricals by the time it prepared the statement.

We can therefore explain the difference between the parties as a TIMING DIFFERENCE, and produce a RECONCILIATION which shows how the difference is made up:

Reconciliation statement

	£
As at 28 February 20XX	
Amount per Southfield statement	5,882.60
Amount per Whitehill purchases ledger	4,527.09
Difference	1,355.51

Explained by: timing difference

Automated payment made, not received as at 28 Feb	1,301.31
Settlement discount taken with payment, not recorded as at 28 Feb	54.20
	1,355.51

WHEN TO PAY SUPPLIER INVOICES

When all the checks have been carried out and it has been determined that the invoice is correct then it must be authorised and passed for payment. Organisations use different methods to determine when invoices should be paid.

Paying by supplier statement

Once the supplier statement has been reconciled to the purchases ledger, in many organisations the statement is used as the means of identifying what amounts should be paid. In other words, payment is only made upon receipt and reconciliation of a supplier's statement of account. Such statements are normally received just after the end of the month and will have been prepared as at the end of the month. Payment will then be made according to the supplier's terms. This means that all invoices, less credit notes, that are more than, say, 30 days old will be paid.

HOW IT WORKS

The following statement is received by Dagwell Enterprises from their supplier Southfield Electricals on 4 December 20XX.

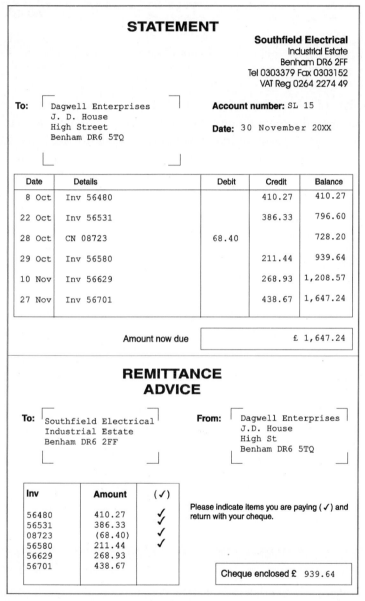

STATEMENT

Southfield Electrical
Industrial Estate
Benham DR6 2FF
Tel 0303379 Fax 0303152
VAT Reg 0264 2274 49

To: Dagwell Enterprises
J. D. House
High Street
Benham DR6 5TQ

Account number: SL 15

Date: 30 November 20XX

Date	Details	Debit	Credit	Balance
8 Oct	Inv 56480		410.27	410.27
22 Oct	Inv 56531		386.33	796.60
28 Oct	CN 08723	68.40		728.20
29 Oct	Inv 56580		211.44	939.64
10 Nov	Inv 56629		268.93	1,208.57
27 Nov	Inv 56701		438.67	1,647.24

Amount now due   £ 1,647.24

REMITTANCE ADVICE

To: Southfield Electrical
Industrial Estate
Benham DR6 2FF

From: Dagwell Enterprises
J.D. House
High St
Benham DR6 5TQ

Inv	Amount	(✓)
56480	410.27	✓
56531	386.33	✓
08723	(68.40)	✓
56580	211.44	✓
56629	268.93	
56701	438.67	

Please indicate items you are paying (✓) and return with your cheque.

Cheque enclosed £ 939.64

If Dagwell Enterprises' policy is to pay all of the invoices dated up to a month before the statement date, it would pay off the following invoices with one payment:

	£
Invoice 56480	410.27
Invoice 56531	386.33
CN 08723	(68.40)
Invoice 56580	211.44
	939.64

The advantage of this method of payment is that only one payment is made each month. However, the main disadvantage is that any settlement discounts offered would be lost, as any payment made would be too late to take advantage of the discount. It also means that a longer period of credit is being taken than the stated 30 days. For example the invoice dated 8 October is not being paid until early December, which is closer to 60 days of credit.

Rather than pay by statement therefore some businesses will make:

- Payment by invoice, or
- Payment on a regular timescale.

Paying by invoice

This system means that a precise payment date for each invoice is set when it has been checked and authorised as ready for payment.

The payment date will depend upon the payment terms of the invoice and whether or not any settlement discount is to be taken. If there is no settlement discount offered then most organisations are likely to take as much credit as possible in order to keep money in their own bank account for as long as possible, thereby earning interest or reducing overdraft interest.

Therefore when the invoice is passed for payment, the invoice date and terms should be checked in order to determine the latest date on which payment should be made.

HOW IT WORKS

If an invoice dated 23 May is received on 26 May and the terms state that payment is due in 30 days then the payment date would be calculated as 22 June (as there are 31 days in May). The payment should reach the supplier on this date so the day for writing the cheque or authorising the automated payment is 20 June. This payment date must then be recorded in a diary system which will show the precise invoices that are due to be paid each day.

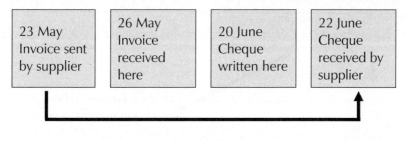

30 days

Task 3

An invoice is received on 14 July. The invoice is dated 9 July and the terms are stated as "net 30 days". Payment is to be made by cheque and posted and this takes three days from writing out the cheque to receipt by the supplier. When should the cheque be written?

Settlement discounts

If a settlement discount is offered on an invoice then there are further considerations in deciding when to make payment.

- Is it the organisation's policy to take settlement discounts? If a settlement discount is taken then obviously a smaller amount is paid to the supplier, but it is paid earlier, meaning that money leaves the organisation's bank account earlier. This reduces any interest receivable on the account or increases any overdraft interest.

- If the policy of the organisation is only to take settlement discounts from some suppliers, depending upon the terms that they offer, is this supplier one of those for which a settlement discount should be taken?

- If the settlement discount is to be taken, how much should the payment be and when should it be made?

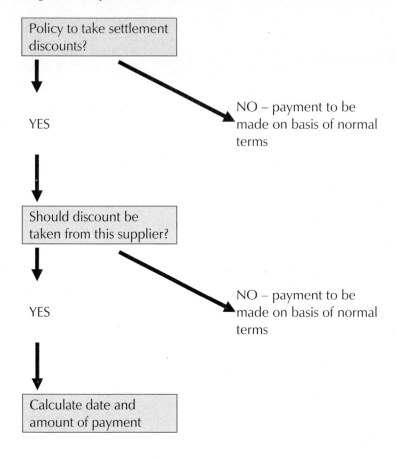

The amount of the payment will be considered a little later in the chapter. Here we will consider the timing of the payment.

HOW IT WORKS

An invoice is received on 10 December and is dated 8 December. The terms show that a settlement discount of 3.5% is offered for payment received within 14 days of the invoice date. Payment is to be made by cheque and posted, which takes two days. When should the cheque be written in order to take advantage of the discount?

The invoice is dated 8 December, so to take advantage of the settlement discount the payment must reach the supplier no later than 22 December. Therefore the cheque should be written on 20 December at the very latest.

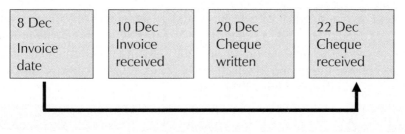

14 days

Task 4

An invoice dated 23 November is received on 25 November. The settlement discount of 4% for payment within ten days of the invoice date is to be taken and the payment will be received by the supplier two days after the cheque is written. What is the latest date that the cheque should be written?

Payment on a regular timescale

In practice, many organisations may make payments on a weekly basis rather than a daily or monthly basis. So, for example, payments may be made every Friday instead of every day. In this case, when an invoice is passed for payment it must be determined which Friday the payment must be paid in order not to exceed the credit period.

HOW IT WORKS

An invoice dated Monday 7 August is received from the supplier on Thursday 10 August. The stated credit terms are 30 days from the invoice date. With 30 days credit the payment should reach the supplier by Wednesday 6 September, so the cheque needs to be written on the previous Friday, 1 September.

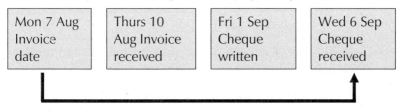

30 days

If payment is made on a weekly basis and a settlement discount is offered, calculations should be made to determine in which week the payment must be made in order to be able validly to take the settlement discount. This must be done promptly or the period in which the discount is valid will pass, no payment will be made and the discount will be lost.

AMOUNT OF THE PAYMENT

As well as making sure that payments are made according to the organisational timescales that are set, the correct amount must be paid.

Settlement discounts

Calculation of the settlement discount to be deducted may be made when the invoice is checked for accuracy as we saw earlier or it may be made at this later stage.

Remember that the settlement discount to be deducted from the invoice total is the discount percentage of the net total on the invoice. The VAT has already been calculated on the basis that the discount will be taken.

HOW IT WORKS

Given below is an extract from one of Whitehill Superstores' invoices:

	£
Goods total	3,000.00
VAT	588.00
Invoice total	3,588.00

Terms 2% settlement discount for payment received within 14 days of the invoice date

The payment that will be made if the discount is taken is calculated as follows:

Step 1   Calculate the discount to be deducted:

$$£3,000.00 \times 2/100 = £60.00$$

Step 2   Deduct the discount from the invoice total to find the amount to be paid:

$$£3,588.00 - £60.00 = £3,528.00$$

Task 5

An invoice is received by your organisation on which a settlement discount of 2.5% is offered. The totals are given below:

	£
Net total	2,000.00
VAT	390.00
Invoice total	2,390.00

Calculate the amount of the payment required if the discount is taken.

£ [   ]

PREPARING A REMITTANCE ADVICE NOTE

We saw earlier that when a supplier sends a statement of account to a customer a tear-off REMITTANCE ADVICE NOTE is often added to the bottom, for the customer to fill in showing the details and amounts of the invoices being paid, less credit notes and settlement discounts. When filling in a remittance advice note – on a statement or generated within the business – and totalling it to find the total payment, care should be taken to ensure that the total is correctly added up.

HOW IT WORKS

The statement of account received by Dagwell Enterprises earlier is shown again.

STATEMENT

Southfield Electrical
Industrial Estate
Benham DR6 2FF
Tel 0303379 Fax 0303152
VAT Reg 0264 2274 49

To: Dagwell Enterprises
J. D. House
High Street
Benham DR6 5TQ

Account number: SL 15

Date: 30 November 20XX

Date	Details	Debit	Credit	Balance
8 Oct	Inv 56480		410.27	410.27
22 Oct	Inv 56531		386.33	796.60
28 Oct	CN 08723	68.40		728.20
29 Oct	Inv 56580		211.44	939.64
10 Nov	Inv 56629		268.93	1,208.57
27 Nov	Inv 56701		438.67	1,647.24

Amount now due | £ 1,647.24

REMITTANCE ADVICE

To: Southfield Electrical
Industrial Estate
Benham DR6 2FF

From: Dagwell Enterprises
J.D. House
High St
Benham DR6 5TQ

Inv	Amount	(✓)
56480	410.27	✓
56531	386.33	✓
08723	(68.40)	✓
56580	211.44	✓
56629	268.93	
56701	438.67	

Please indicate items you are paying (✓) and return with your cheque.

Cheque enclosed £ 939.64

The invoices and credit notes that are being settled by this payment are ticked and then added up and the total entered in the "cheque enclosed" section. If the addition is incorrect then the amount paid will also be incorrect.

AUTHORISATION LIMITS

Most organisations have a system whereby different levels of accounts department employees deal with different amounts of payments. When organising the payments for your organisation you should always be aware of your authorisation limits and know to whom to pass payments that exceed that limit.

HOW IT WORKS

You are in charge of scheduling payments to credit suppliers and you have been set an authorisation limit of £200. Any payments to suppliers up to this amount can therefore be arranged by you. If, however, a payment is due to a supplier of £500 then a higher level of accounts department employee, such as a manager, will be required to authorise this amount for payment.

CHAPTER OVERVIEW

- The main methods of ordering goods are in writing, by fax, over the telephone and over the Internet

- Whatever method of ordering is used, there must be some form of evidence of the goods ordered as this will be needed later when the goods and then the invoice are received

- When the goods are received they will normally be accompanied by a delivery note which must be checked and signed as evidence that the stated quantity of goods was delivered

- On receipt of goods many organisations complete an internal document, the goods received note, detailing the quantity and condition of the goods received

- The accounts department opens a file for each purchase which will include the purchase quotation, the purchase order, the delivery note and the goods received note

- If goods have to be returned to the supplier a returns note may be issued, formally requesting a credit note from the supplier for the returned goods

- When the invoice is received it must first be checked to the purchase order to ensure that the goods were ordered and to the delivery note and GRN to ensure that they were received

- When any related credit note is received this should be filed with the invoice awaiting payment

- All of the calculations on a supplier's invoice should be checked including the deduction of trade discount, any bulk discount, the calculation of total price from quantity and unit price, the additions and the VAT calculation

- Credit notes received should be checked in exactly the same manner

- When invoices for services are received there will be no delivery note or GRN but evidence must be sought that the service has been provided and that the amount charged is reasonable or the agreed amount

- When all of the checks have been carried out and it has been determined that the invoice is correct then it must be authorised and passed for payment

- At this point it may be the organisation's policy for the amount of any settlement discount offered to be calculated – this is the given percentage of the net total of the invoice

- The invoice will probably be coded at this stage to indicate the supplier and the type of goods or services using the supplier code and some element of the product code

CHAPTER OVERVIEW cont'd

- At regular intervals it is likely that the organisation may receive statements from suppliers showing the amount currently due – this may include a tear-off remittance advice which should be returned with the payment indicating which invoices have been paid

Keywords

Purchase order – the written document sent from the buyer to the seller detailing the goods that are being ordered and the agreed price

Delivery note – the document sent by the seller with the goods detailing which goods, and in what quantities, are being sent

Goods received note – an internal document completed by the buyer on receipt of the goods showing the quantity and condition of the goods received

Returns note – the document sent by the purchaser to the seller detailing the goods returned and the reason for their return

Credit note – document stating that a certain amount has been credited to the buyer's account

Invoice – a document that clearly sets out what money is owed by a named trade receivable to a named trade payable in respect of particular goods or services

Reconciliation – a statement showing how any difference owing between parties is made up

Remittance advice note – a document setting out exactly how a payment is made up (ie the invoices/credit notes that it is paying/netting off)

Reconciling – process of checking a suppliers statement of account with organisational records and finding reasons for any discrepancies

Timing difference – reason for a variance in a reconciliation – for example, a payment has been made but has not yet reached the supplier's account when the statement is prepared

TEST YOUR LEARNING

Test 1

Using the picklist below, identify which type of document would be used for the following purposes.

To accompany goods being returned to a supplier	
To record for internal purposes the quantity of goods received	
To request payment from a purchaser of goods	
To order goods from a supplier	
To accompany payment to a supplier	

Picklist:

Delivery note
Returns note
Quotation
Remittance advice note
Invoice
Credit note
Goods received note
Purchase order

Test 2

What is the main problem with placing an order for goods over the telephone and how can this be overcome?

Test 3

Given below are an invoice and credit note received by A J Hammond and the related purchase order, delivery note and goods received note. Check the invoice and credit note thoroughly and note any problems that there might be.

INVOICE

P T Cards
Foram Road
Winnesh DR3 4TP
Tel 0611223 Fax 0611458
VAT Reg 0661 3247 98

To:
A.J. Hammond
Brockham Park Estate
Winnesh DR3 2XJ

Invoice number: 46298

Date/tax point: 5 Oct 20XX

Order number: 304051

Account number: H03

Quantity	Description	Product code	Unit amount £	Total £
200	Birthday Cards	TN451	0.89	178.00
600	Christmas Cards	SJ106	0.45	270.00
100	Get Well Cards	GW444	0.33	33.00

Net total	481.00
VAT	96.20
Invoice total	577.20

Terms
E & OE

CREDIT NOTE

P T Cards
Foram Road
Winnesh DR3 4TP
Tel 0611223 Fax 0611458
VAT Reg 0661 3247 98

Credit note to:
A.J. Hammond
Brockham Park Estate
Winnesh DR3 2XJ

Credit note number: 31313
Date/tax point: 10 Oct 20XX
Order number: 304051
Account number: H03

Quantity	Description	Product code	Unit amount	Total
			£	£
30	Get Well Cards	GW444	0.25	7.50

Net total	7.50
VAT	1.50
Gross total	9.00

Reason for credit note:
Not ordered

PURCHASE ORDER

A J HAMMOND
Brockham Park Estate
Winnesh DR3 2XJ

To: P.T.Cards
Foram Road
Winnesh DR3 4TP

Number: 304051

Date: 13 Sept 20XX

Delivery address: As above

Product code	Quantity	Description	Price (£)
SJ106	600	Christmas Cards	0.45
GW444	70	Get well Cards	0.33
TN451	200	Birthday Cards	0.89

Authorised by: _P T Thomas_ **Date:** _13 Sept 20XX_

DELIVERY NOTE

P T Cards
Foram Road
Winnesh DR3 4TP
Tel 0611223 Fax 0611458

Delivery address:

A.J.Hammond
Brockham Park Estate
Winnesh DR3 2XJ

Number: 21690

Date: 20 Sept 20XX

Order number: 304051

Product code	Quantity	Description
SJ106	600	Christmas Cards
GW444	100	Get Well Cards
TN451	200	Birthday Cards

Received by: [Signature] *J T Turner*   **Print name:** *J T TURNER*

Date: *20 Sept 20XX*

GOODS RECEIVED NOTE

A J Hammond
Brockham Park Estate
Winnesh DR3 2XJ

Supplier:

GRN number: 27420

Date: 21 Sept 20XX

Order number: 304051

Delivery Note No: 21690

Quantity	Description	Product code
200	Birthday Cards	TN 451
100	Get Well Cards	GW 444
600	Christmas Cards	SJ 106

Received by: *P Darren*

Checked by: *D Gough*

Comments: *All in good condition*

Test 4

Given below are three invoices received from suppliers by Whitehill Superstores.

An extract from the supplier code listing is given:

Bass Engineers   PL 13

Southfield Electrical   PL 20

Herne Industries   PL 15

Today's date is 20 October. You are required to record the invoice details in the Purchases Day Book and also total the Purchases Day Book.

Purchases Day Book

Date	Supplier	Invoice number	Supplier code	Invoice total £	VAT £	Net £
		Total				

INVOICE

Herne Industries
Fuller House
Bean Park
Benham DR6 3PQ
Tel 0303226 Fax 0303582
VAT Reg 0624 3361 29

To: Whitehill Superstores
28, Whitehill Park
Benham DR6 5LM

Invoice number: 46121

Date/tax point: 16 Oct 20XX

Order number: 32216

Account number: SL 23

Quantity	Description	Product code	Unit amount £	Total £
3	Komax Camcorder	KC410	240.00	720.00

Net total	720.00
VAT	144.00
Invoice total	864.00

Terms
Net 30 days
E & OE

INVOICE

Bass Engineers
Bass House
Parrish DR3 2FL
Tel 0462333 Fax 0462334
VAT Reg 2016 2131 87

To: Whitehill Superstores
28, Whitehill Park
Benham DR6 5LM

Invoice number: 663211

Date/tax point: 15 Oct 20XX

Order number: 32213

Account number: W15

Quantity	Description	Product code	Unit amount £	Total £
16	Standard lamps	33116	24.00	384.00

Net total	384.00
VAT	76.80
Invoice total	460.80

Terms
Net 30 days
E & OE

INVOICE

Southfield Electrical
Industrial Estate
Benham DR6 2FF
Tel 0303379 Fax 0303152
VAT Reg 0264 2274 49

To: Whitehill Superstores
28, Whitehill Park
Benham DR6 5LM

Invoice number: 56521

Date/tax point: 12 Oct 20xx

Order number: 3226

Account number: SL 44

Quantity	Description	Product code	Unit amount £	Total £
6	Zanpoint Freezer	6540	310.00	1,860.00
Less:	10% discount			186.00

Net total	1,674.00
VAT	321.40
Invoice total	1,995.40

Terms
4% discount for settlement within 10 days, otherwise 30 days net
E & OE

Test 5

Today's date is 20 October. Given below are two credit notes received by Whitehill Superstores. Enter the details of these credit notes into the Purchases Returns Day Book and then total the Day Book – use the account references from the previous question.

Purchases Returns Day Book

Date	Supplier	Credit note number	Supplier code	Credit note total £	VAT £	Net £
		Total				

CREDIT NOTE

SOUTHFIELD ELECTRICAL
INDUSTRIAL ESTATE
Benham DR6 2FF
Tel 0303379 Fax 0303152
VAT Reg 0264 2274 49

Invoice to:

    Whitehill Superstores
    28 Whitehill Park
    Benham DR6 5LM

Credit note number: 08702

Date/tax point: 16 Oct 20XX

Order number   32217

Account number: SL 44

Quantity	Description	Product code	Unit amount	Total
			£	£
2	Temax Coffee maker	9130	50.00	100.00

Net total	100.00
VAT	20.00
Gross total	120.00

Reason for credit note:

    Not ordered by customer

CREDIT NOTE

HERNE INDUSTRIES
Fuller House
Bean Park
Benham DR6 3PQ
Tel 0303226 Fax 0303582
VAT Reg 0624 3361 29

Invoice to:		**Credit note number:**	CN 4502
Whitehill Superstores		**Date/tax point:**	17 Oct 20XX
28 Whitehill Park		**Order number**	32221
Benham DR6 5LM		**Account number:**	SL 23

Quantity	Description	Product code	Unit amount	Total
			£	£
1	Kemax Camera	KC450	110.00	110.00
		Net total		110.00
		VAT		22.00
		Gross total		132.00

Reason for credit note:

Wrong items

Test 6

Given below is a statement from one of your organisation's suppliers and an attached blank remittance advice. You are told that all the May invoices less credit notes are to be paid and that there is no settlement discount offered by this supplier. Today's date is 5 July 20XX.

Complete the remittance advice.

STATEMENT

Fishpool Supplies
280 Main Road
Winnish DR2 5TL
Tel 0411226 Fax 041126
VAT Reg 0611 2383 58

To:
Tryprint Traders
Barnsgate Industrial Park
Fretton PT7 2XY

Account number: SL 48

Date: 30 June 20XX

Date	Details	Debit	Credit	Balance
7 May	Inv 61234		401.23	401.23
14 May	Inv 61287		226.40	627.63
20 May	Inv 61299		106.68	734.31
28 May	CN C4361	16.48		717.83
6 June	Inv 61340		430.16	1,147.99
19 June	Inv 61388		269.73	1,417.72

Amount now due   £ 1,417.72

REMITTANCE ADVICE

To:
Fishpool Supplies
280, Main Rd
Winnish DR2 5TL

From:
Tryprint Traders
Barnsgate Ind Park
Fretton PT7 2XY

Invoices	Amount £

Cheque enclosed £

Test 7

The following transactions all took place on 30 November and have been entered into the Purchases Day Book as shown below. No entries have yet been made into the ledger system.

Purchases Day Book

Date 20XX	Details	Invoice number	Total £	VAT @ 20% £	Net £
30 Nov	Lindell Co	24577	2,136	356	1,780
30 Nov	Harris Rugs	829	5,256	876	4,380
30 Nov	Kinshasa Music	10/235	2,796	466	2,330
30 Nov	Calnan Ltd	9836524	2,292	382	1,910
	Totals		12,480	2,080	10,400

What will be the entries in the purchases ledger?

Purchases ledger

Account name	Amount £	Left side of account ✓	Right side of account ✓	Details in account

Test 8

Purchase invoices have been received and partially entered in the analysed Purchases Day Book, as shown below.

(a) Complete the entries in the Purchases Day Book by inserting the appropriate figures for each invoice.

(b) Total the last five columns of the Purchases Day Book.

Purchases Day Book

Date 20XX	Details	Invoice number	Total £	VAT @ 20% £	Net £	Purchases £	Expenses £
30 Nov	Papford & Co	29000	3,180				2,650
30 Nov	Havelock Beauty	120/22		196		980	
30 Nov	Hareston Ltd	7638		1,564		7,820	
	Totals						

Test 9

A supply of printer paper has been delivered to Wendlehurst Trading by Patel Stationery. The purchase order sent from Wendlehurst Trading, and the invoice from Patel Stationery, are shown below.

Wendlehurst Trading
Purchase Order No. PO89346

To: Patel Stationery

Date: 7 Dec 20XX

Please supply 100 reams printer paper product code PAP6735
Purchase price: £80 per box of 20 reams, plus VAT
Discount: less 12.5% trade discount, as agreed.

Patel Stationery
Invoice No. 109273

Wendlehurst Trading

10 Dec 20XX

100 reams printer paper product code PAP6735 @ £4 each	£400.00
Trade discount	(£40.00)
Net amount	£360.00
VAT @ 20%	£ 72.00
Total	£432.00

Terms: 30 days net

Check the invoice against the purchase order and answer the following questions.

	Yes ✓	No ✓
Has the correct purchase price of the printer paper been charged?		
Has the correct trade discount been applied?		
What would be the VAT amount charged if the invoice was correct?	£	
What would be the total amount charged if the invoice was correct?	£	

chapter 6:
DOUBLE ENTRY BOOKKEEPING

chapter coverage 📖

Now that we have considered the preparation and authorisation of invoices and credit notes, and their entry into the books of prime entry and sales/purchases ledgers, in this chapter we turn to the basics of double entry bookkeeping.

The topics covered are:

- ✐ The principles of double entry bookkeeping
- ✐ The accounting equation
- ✐ Recording transactions in ledger accounts
- ✐ General rules for double entry bookkeeping
- ✐ Balancing ledger accounts
- ✐ Distinguishing capital and revenue expenditure
- ✐ Double entry for credit sales and purchases in the general ledger

DOUBLE ENTRY BOOKKEEPING

Accounting is based upon a system of DOUBLE ENTRY BOOKKEEPING, the fundamental principle of which is:

Each and every transaction has two effects

This principle actually incorporates three related principles, two of which we encountered very briefly in Chapter 1 of this Text and which we shall look at further now.

PRINCIPLES OF DOUBLE ENTRY BOOKKEEPING

The three main principles that underlie the practice of recording transactions in a double entry bookkeeping system are:

(a) The SEPARATE ENTITY CONCEPT – the owner of a business is a completely separate entity to the business itself

(b) There is an ACCOUNTING EQUATION which always holds true:

ASSETS minus LIABILITIES equals CAPITAL

(c) The DUAL EFFECT of transactions – each and every transaction that a business undertakes has two effects on the business

THE ACCOUNTING EQUATION

To understand the accounting equation a little better you need to know more about its different elements:

- ASSETS are items that the business owns, such as cash and machinery and amounts owed to the business by trade receivables.

- LIABILITIES are amounts that are owed to other parties, such as loans, overdrafts and amounts owed to trade payables.

- CAPITAL is the amount that is owed by the business to its owner as a separate entity. Capital at any point in time is made up of:

  - Initial capital introduced, plus
  - The business's INCOME, less
  - The business's EXPENSES, less
  - The owner's DRAWINGS of cash or goods for their own use

- The main sources of INCOME for a business will be from sales of goods and services, but may also include interest paid to the business by its bank and other sundry income such as rent received from tenants, and commission received from acting as an agent

- The main EXPENSES of the business will be the goods that it purchases for resale as well as the other ongoing costs of running the business such as wages to employees (**not** the owner), rent paid for its premises, utilities and stationery.

HOW IT WORKS

We will look at the initial transactions of a small business to illustrate the dual effect, and eventually the accounting equation. For the moment we shall assume that all transactions related to cash are passed through the business's bank account.

- Ben Charles sets up in business on 1 May by paying £10,000 into a business bank account from his redundancy money as the business's initial capital.

Cash into the business of £10,000	The business 'owes' Ben his £10,000 capital

- Ben buys some goods for resale for £1,000 in cash

Purchases of £1,000 have been made	Cash of £1,000 is paid out

- Ben buys some goods for resale for £2,000 on credit

Purchases of £2,000 have been made	A trade payable for £2,000 exists

- Ben pays rent for premises of £600 in cash

A rent expense of £600 has been incurred	Cash of £600 is paid out

- Sales of £1,500 for cash are made by selling some of the goods

Cash has increased by £1,500	Sales of £1,500 have been made

151

- Sales of £1,800 are made on credit

| A trade receivable for £1,800 exists | Sales of £1,800 have been made |

- Ben purchases a computer to help with the accounting process at a cost of £1,000 and pays for this by cheque

| The business now has a computer worth £1,000 that it will keep | Cash has decreased by £1,000 |

- Ben buys computer disks and other stationery for £200 by cheque

| An expense of £200 is incurred | Cash is decreased by £200 |

- Ben takes out £500 from the business for his own living expenses

| Drawings of £500 have been made | Cash is decreased by £500 |

- Ben pays his trade payable £1,500

| The amount of the trade payable is reduced by £1,500 | Cash is reduced by £1,500 |

- Ben's credit customer pays £1,750 by cheque

| Cash is increased by £1,750 | The amount of the trade receivable is reduced by £1,750 |

- Ben agrees with his credit customer that, as it paid so quickly, Ben would deduct £50 from the amount owed as settlement discount

| Ben has suffered an expense (discount allowed) of £50 | The amount of the trade receivable is reduced by £50 |

Task 1

What are the two effects of the following transactions?

(a) Purchase of goods on credit

    Increase expense

    Increase sales

    Increase trade payable

    Increase trade receivable

(b) Sale of goods on credit

    Increase expense

    Increase sales

    Increase trade payable

    Increase trade receivable

(c) Receipt of money for sale of goods on credit

    Increase cash

    Decrease cash

    Decrease trade receivable

    Increase trade receivable

(d) Payment to a trade payable for purchase of goods on credit

    Increase cash

    Decrease cash

    Decrease trade payable

    Increase trade payable

LEDGER ACCOUNTS

Both sides of each transaction need to be recorded in the organisation's accounting records.

The traditional method of recording these transactions is in a LEDGER ACCOUNT in the organisation's GENERAL LEDGER.

153

- 'Ledger' simply means 'book'
- The general ledger is the accounting record which forms the complete set of ledger accounts for the organisation

Each type of transaction has a ledger account in the general ledger. An illustration of a ledger account follows below (they are often called T accounts because of how they look):

		Title				**GL 000**	
Date	Ref	Details	£	Date	Ref	Details	£

You have already seen ledger accounts like this in relation to the sales and purchases ledger in Chapters 3 to 5. It is now time to make the structure of a ledger account explicit. Each one has:

- Two sides, because each transaction has two effects
    - The left-hand side is the DEBIT side
    - The right-hand side is the CREDIT side

- A title, which explains which transaction it is recording, eg sales, purchases

The fundamental principle of double entry bookkeeping is that:

Each and every transaction has two effects

So for every transaction that a business makes there must be:

- A debit entry in one ledger account and
- An equal and opposite credit entry in another ledger account

The skill that you must acquire is to know which accounts to put the debit and credit entries into.

Note that as well as a title, general ledger accounts also have a general ledger code – in this case GL 000. As with customer and supplier codes in the sales and purchases ledgers, a general ledger code makes it much easier to identify which account should be written up, and allows for easy cross-referencing to where the other side of the entry has been made.

GENERAL RULES FOR DOUBLE ENTRY BOOKKEEPING

There are some general rules for double entry bookkeeping which can help you to decide where debit and credit entries should be made:

- If cash, which is an asset, comes into the business, then the Bank account is always debited – therefore some other account must be credited:

    INCREASE IN ASSET = DEBIT ENTRY

- If cash is paid out of the business (an asset has decreased), then the Bank account is always credited – therefore some other account must be debited:

    DECREASE IN ASSET = CREDIT ENTRY

- An increase in liabilities – eg a bank loan – is always recorded on the credit side of the liability account:

    INCREASE IN LIABILITY = CREDIT ENTRY
    DECREASE IN LIABILITY = DEBIT ENTRY

- An increase in capital is always recorded on the credit side of the capital account:

    INCREASE IN CAPITAL = CREDIT ENTRY
    DECREASE IN CAPITAL = DEBIT ENTRY

- An increase in expenses is always a debit entry in the expenses account:

    INCREASE IN EXPENSE = DEBIT ENTRY
    DECREASE IN EXPENSE = CREDIT ENTRY

- An increase in income is always a credit entry in the income account:

    INCREASE IN INCOME = CREDIT ENTRY
    DECREASE IN INCOME = DEBIT ENTRY

Asset account eg bank

	£		£
Debit entry	+	Credit entry	–

Liability account eg bank loan

	£		£
Debit entry	–	Credit entry	+

Capital account

	£		£
Debit entry	–	Credit entry	+

Expense account

Details	£	Details	£
Debit entry	+	Credit entry	−

Income account

Details	£	Details	£
Debit entry	−	Credit entry	+

HOW IT WORKS

We will now return to Ben Charles's business and enter each of his initial transactions into general ledger accounts. For this example we will simplify the ledger accounts slightly, not worrying about the date or any reference, just concentrating on the debit and the credit entry, and entering the details for each transaction, which is the name of the account to which the other side of the entry is made.

Ben sets up in business on 1 May by paying £10,000 into a business bank account

Cash has come into the business therefore the Bank account must be debited. The money paid in is from the owner of the business. It is therefore capital of the business so the credit entry is to the capital account.

Bank account

Details	£	Details	£
Capital	10,000		

Capital account

Details	£	Details	£
		Bank	10,000

Note how the details for each entry shows where the other side of the entry is.

In terms of the accounting equation, we see at this point that:

ASSETS (£10,000) − LIABILITIES (£0) = CAPITAL (£10,000)

Ben buys some goods for resale for £1,000 in cash

Cash is going out of the business so the Bank account must be credited.

The payment was for goods for resale which are known as purchases, an expense account, so this is the account that must be debited.

Bank account

Details	£	Details	£
Capital	10,000	Purchases	1,000

Purchases account

Details	£	Details	£
Bank	1,000		

Ben buys some goods for resale for £2,000 on credit

Again, these goods are purchases so the purchases account must be debited.

The transaction is not for cash this time so there is no entry into the Bank account, instead the credit entry is to a trade payables account (a trade payable is another form of liability, so an increase is always a credit entry as with the bank loan account that we saw above).

Purchases account

Details	£	Details	£
Bank	1,000		
Trade payables	2,000		

Trade payables account

Details	£	Details	£
		Purchases	2,000

Ben pays rent for premises of £600 in cash

Cash out of the business; therefore credit the Bank account.

The rent is an expense of the business so the rent account must be debited – an increase in expenses is always a debit entry in the expense ledger accounts.

Bank account

Details	£	Details	£
Capital	10,000	Purchases	1,000
		Rent	600

Rent account

Details	£	Details	£
Bank	600		

Sales of £1,500 for cash are made by selling some of the goods

Cash is coming into the business from these sales therefore debit the Bank account.

The credit is to the sales account – remember that an increase in income is always a credit entry.

Bank account

Details	£	Details	£
Capital	10,000	Purchases	1,000
Sales	1,500	Rent	600

Sales account

Details	£	Details	£
		Bank	1,500

Sales of £1,800 are made on credit

Again, we have a sale so the sales account must be credited.

This time however there is no cash coming in so it is not the Bank account that is debited, instead the debit entry is made in a trade receivables account – remember that an increase in an asset such as a trade receivable is always a debit entry.

Sales account

Details	£	Details	£
		Bank	1,500
		Trade receivables	1,800

Trade receivables account

Details	£	Details	£
Sales	1,800		

Ben purchases a computer to help with the accounting process at a cost of £1,000 and pays for this by cheque

Cash goes out of the business, so credit the Bank account.

An asset such as a computer that will be owned for some time by the business – known as a NON-CURRENT ASSET – has been purchased so a debit is required in a non-current asset account. Remember that increases in assets are always debit entries.

Bank account

Details	£	Details	£
Capital	10,000	Purchases	1,000
Sales	1,500	Rent	600
		Non-current asset	1,000

Non-current asset account

Details	£	Details	£
Bank	1,000		

Ben buys computer disks and other stationery for £200 by cheque

Cash goes out of the business, so credit the Bank account.

The stationery and disks are an expense to the business so a stationery account will be opened and debited.

Bank account

Details	£	Details	£
Capital	10,000	Purchases	1,000
Sales	1,500	Rent	600
		Non-current asset	1,000
		Stationery	200

Stationery account

Details	£	Details	£
Bank	200		

Ben takes out £500 from the business for his own living expenses

Cash goes out of the business, so credit the Bank account.

This is the owner taking money out of the business which is known as DRAWINGS, so a drawings account is debited.

Bank account

Details	£	Details	£
Capital	10,000	Purchases	1,000
Sales	1,500	Rent	600
		Non-current asset	1,000
		Stationery	200
		Drawings	500

Drawings account

Details	£	Details	£
Bank	500		

Ben pays his trade payable £1,500

Cash goes out of the business, so credit the Bank account.

The money is being paid to his trade payable therefore it is reducing his liability to that trade payable. The trade payables account is debited to reflect this.

Bank account

Details	£	Details	£
Capital	10,000	Purchases	1,000
Sales	1,500	Rent	600
		Non-current asset	1,000
		Stationery	200
		Drawings	500
		Trade payables	1,500

Trade payables account

Details	£	Details	£
Bank	1,500	Purchases	2,000

Ben's credit customer pays £1,750 by cheque

This is cash being received into the business so the Bank account is debited.

The credit entry is to the trade receivables account, as this receipt is reducing the amount that the trade receivable owes the business.

Bank account

Details	£	Details	£
Capital	10,000	Purchases	1,000
Sales	1,500	Rent	600
Trade receivables	1,750	Non-current asset	1,000
		Stationery	200
		Drawings	500
		Trade payables	1,500

Trade receivables account

Details	£	Details	£
Sales	1,800	Bank	1,750

> Ben agrees with his credit customer that, as it paid so quickly, Ben would deduct £50 from the amount owed as settlement discount

There is no cash being received into or paid out from the business so the Bank account is not affected. There is a credit entry to the trade receivables account, as the settlement discount reduces the amount owed to Ben by the customer. The debit entry is made to a special expense ledger account, called DISCOUNTS ALLOWED.

Discounts allowed

Details	£	Details	£
Trade receivables	50		

Trade receivables account

Details	£	Details	£
Sales	1,800	Bank	1,750
		Discounts allowed	50

Task 2

For each of the following transactions, state which account should be debited and which account credited by using the account names from the picklist:

(a)   Purchase of goods on credit

Account name	Debit	Credit

(b)   Sale of goods on credit

Account name	Debit	Credit

(c)   Receipt of money for sale of goods on credit

Account name	Debit	Credit

> **Picklist:**
> Bank
> Trade payables
> Trade receivables
> Sales
> Purchases

BALANCING THE LEDGER ACCOUNTS

Once all of the accounting entries have been put into the ledger accounts for a period then it is likely that the owner or managers of a business will want to know certain things such as how much is there in the bank account, how many sales have there been in the period, how much do we owe our trade payables at the end of the period etc?

These questions can be answered by balancing the ledger accounts.

HOW IT WORKS

We will illustrate the balancing process by using Ben Charles's ledger accounts for his initial period of trading. Let's start with the Bank account.

Bank account

Details	£	Details	£
Capital	10,000	Purchases	1,000
Sales	1,500	Rent	600
Trade receivables	1,750	Non-current asset	1,000
		Stationery	200
		Drawings	500
		Trade payables	1,500

Step 1   Total both the debit and the credit columns, making a note of the totals for each.

Debit column total £13,250
Credit column total £4,800

Step 2   Put the largest of the two totals as the column total for both the debit and credit columns, leaving at least one empty line at the bottom of each column.

162

Bank account

Details	£	Details	£
Capital	10,000	Purchases	1,000
Sales	1,500	Rent	600
Trade receivables	1,750	Non-current asset	1,000
		Stationery	200
		Drawings	500
		Trade payables	1,500
	13,250		13,250

Step 3 At the bottom of the column with the smaller actual total, put in the figure that makes the column total add to the larger figure. In this case, in the credit column, put in £(13,250 – 4,800) =£8,450. This is called the BALANCE CARRIED DOWN (Bal c/d).

Bank account

Details	£	Details	£
Capital	10,000	Purchases	1,000
Sales	1,500	Rent	600
Trade receivables	1,750	Non-current asset	1,000
		Stationery	200
		Drawings	500
		Trade payables	1,500
		Balance c/d	8,450
	13,250		13,250

Step 4 Show this balancing figure on the opposite side of the account below the total and describe it as the BALANCE BROUGHT DOWN (Bal b/d).

Bank account

Details	£	Details	£
Capital	10,000	Purchases	1,000
Sales	1,500	Rent	600
Trade receivables	1,750	Non-current asset	1,000
		Stationery	200
		Drawings	500
		Trade payables	1,500
		Balance c/d	8,450
	13,250		13,250
Balance b/d	8,450		

The brought down balance is showing us that we have an asset (a debit balance) of £8,450 of cash in the bank account.

Now we will balance all of the other accounts for Ben Charles in the same way. Note that if we include dates in the ledger accounts, the date of the balance brought down is one day after the date of the balance carried down.

Capital account

Details	£	Details	£
		Bank	10,000

When an account has only one entry, like the capital account, there is no need for the balancing exercise as this single entry is the balance ie, a credit balance of £10,000.

Purchases account

Details	£	Details	£
Bank	1,000		
Trade payables	2,000	Balance c/d	3,000
	3,000		3,000
Balance b/d	3,000		

This shows that purchases totalled £3,000 in the period.

Trade payables account

Details	£	Details	£
Bank	1,500	Purchases	2,000
Balance c/d	500		
	2,000		2,000
		Balance b/d	500

This shows that Ben still owes his trade payable £500 at the end of the period.

Rent account

Details	£	Details	£
Bank	600		

This shows that the rent expense for the period was £600.

Sales account

Details	£	Details	£
		Bank	1,500
Balance c/d	3,300	Trade receivables	1,800
	3,300		3,300
		Balance b/d	3,300

This shows that sales totalled £3,300 in the period.

Trade receivables account

Details	£	Details	£
Sales	1,800	Bank	1,750
		Discounts allowed	50
		Balance c/d	0
	1,800		1,800
Balance b/d	0		

This shows that Ben's trade receivable owes nothing at the end of the period.

Non-current asset account

Details	£	Details	£
Bank	1,000		

This is simply the balance on the non-current asset account showing that the business has a non-current asset that cost £1,000.

Stationery account

Details	£	Details	£
Bank	200		

The stationery expense in the period was £200.

Drawings account

Details	£	Details	£
Bank	500		

This shows that the owner's drawings for the period totalled £500.

Discounts allowed

Details	£	Details	£
Trade receivables	50		

This shows us that the total expense of discounts allowed in the period was £50.

Task 3

Balance the following ledger account, showing clearly the balances carried down and brought down.

Trade receivables

Details	£	Details	£
Sales	2,600	Bank	1,800
Sales	1,400	Bank	1,200
Sales	3,700	Bank	2,000
Sales	1,300		
Total		Total	

What does the balance represent?

The amount owed by trade receivables

The amount owed to trade receivables

DOUBLE ENTRY AND THE ACCOUNTING EQUATION

We saw above that the accounting equation is closely linked with the dual effect and therefore double entry.

ASSETS minus LIABILITIES equals CAPITAL

So let's see if the accounting equation holds true for Ben Charles now that we have done all the double entry for the period and know the balances on all his ledger accounts.

HOW IT WORKS

Bearing in mind that the capital side of the accounting equation comprises initial capital plus income less purchases, expenses and drawings, we can slot all the balances into place:

Assets	£	Liabilities	£	Capital	£
Bank	8,450	Trade payables	500	Capital	10,000
Trade receivables	0			Purchases	(3,000)
Non-current asset	1,000			Rent	(600)
				Sales	3,300
				Stationery	(200)
				Drawings	(500)
				Discounts allowed	(50)
Total assets	9,450	Total liabilities	500	Total capital	8,950

We can see that the accounting equation holds:

ASSETS minus LIABILITIES equals CAPITAL

£9,450 minus £500 equals £8,950

We can be confident therefore, that we have followed the rules of double entry properly.

CAPITAL AND REVENUE EXPENDITURE

Most of the payments that a business makes, both cash and credit transactions, are for purchases of items for manufacture or resale, or wages, or for expenses of the business. These are called REVENUE EXPENDITURE because they are deducted from revenue or income in order to calculate the profit made by the business in a single period such as a year. They are essentially short-term in nature, being purchased and used up all within the period.

Remember though that Ben Charles bought a computer which he planned to use in the business for some time. When a business buys an asset which is for long-term use in the business over a number of periods, such as machinery, property, cars, fixtures and fittings, and computers, these are known as NON-CURRENT ASSETS. The expenditure on these non-current assets is known as CAPITAL EXPENDITURE.

CAPITAL AND REVENUE INCOME

A similar distinction can be made in relation to income. Sales of goods and services, on credit and for cash, are short-term (made and paid within one period only) and are classified as REVENUE INCOME. Other types of REVENUE INCOME include interest received from the bank, commission receipts and rental income. The only type of CAPITAL INCOME that you need to be aware of is income received when a non-current asset such as machinery is sold.

Task 4

Identify whether each of these items is capital expenditure, revenue expenditure, capital income or revenue income.

	Revenue expenditure	Revenue income	Capital expenditure	Capital income
Sale of goods to credit customers				
Cash sales				
Sale of van				
Purchase of goods for resale				
Purchase of building				
Purchase of coffee for office from petty cash				

DOUBLE ENTRY FOR CREDIT SALES IN GENERAL LEDGER

The example of Ben Charles shows us most of the double entries in the general ledger that need to be made for credit sales transactions (which we processed in Chapter 4). In addition, you should note that the double entry for a credit note to a customer is the reverse of that for an invoice, but instead of reversing the sale in the ledger account for sales, the entry is made in a special SALES RETURNS LEDGER ACCOUNT.

The following table summarises the double entries in the general ledger for credit sales transactions:

Transaction	Ledger account to DEBIT	Ledger account to CREDIT
Invoice for a credit sale	Trade receivables	Sales
Credit note for a return	Sales returns	Trade receivables
Cash received	Bank	Trade receivables
Settlement discount allowed	Discounts allowed (an expense account)	Trade receivables

DOUBLE ENTRY FOR CREDIT PURCHASES IN GENERAL LEDGER

Again the example of Ben Charles shows us most of the double entries in the general ledger that need to be made for credit purchases transactions (which we processed in Chapter 5). In addition, you should note that:

- The double entry for a credit note from a supplier is the reverse of that for an invoice, but instead of reversing the purchase in the ledger account for purchases, the entry is made in a special PURCHASES RETURNS LEDGER ACCOUNT

- The double entry for a settlement discount that a supplier has let the business deduct is the opposite of the entry made in relation to discounts allowed, with the credit entry being in the DISCOUNTS RECEIVED LEDGER ACCOUNT

The following table summarises the double entries in the general ledger for credit purchases transactions:

Transaction	Ledger account to DEBIT	Ledger account to CREDIT
Invoice for a purchase	Purchases	Trade payables
Credit note for a return	Trade payables	Purchases returns
Cash paid	Trade payables	Bank
Settlement discount received	Trade payables	Discounts received (an income account)

TYPES OF LEDGER

The ledger accounts that we have been considering so far in this chapter are all kept together in one LEDGER or book. This is known as the GENERAL LEDGER (or sometimes nominal ledger or main ledger).

There are also two other types of ledger, known as the SUBSIDIARY LEDGERS. These are the SALES LEDGER and the PURCHASES LEDGER.

- The sales ledger is a collection of ledger accounts for each individual trade receivable of the business.

- The purchases ledger is a collection of ledger accounts for each individual trade payable of the business.

We have already come across the sales ledger and purchases ledger in previous chapters. We will look at how these subsidiary ledgers and the general ledger interact, and how in practice transactions are posted to these ledgers, in this and the following two chapters.

HOW IT WORKS

A business which is not registered for VAT has three credit customers, A, B and C. The following transactions occur with them during a period.

Sales to credit customers:

	Invoice number	£
A	78346	400
B	78347	600
C	78348	500

The double entry in the general ledger for a sale on credit is:

- To credit **sales** (if the business was registered for VAT the VAT account would also be credited) and

- To debit what we have so far called the trade receivables account, but which in practice and in the assessment is called the SALES LEDGER CONTROL ACCOUNT (because it reflects the total of all the accounts in the sales ledger).

Therefore the double entry in the general ledger will be as follows (note that under 'details' you include the name of the account that takes the other side of the entry).

General ledger

Sales account

Details	£	Details	£
		Sales ledger control	400
		Sales ledger control	600
		Sales ledger control	500

Sales ledger control account

Details	£	Details	£
Sales	400		
Sales	600		
Sales	500		

However, this sales ledger control account gives no detail of the individual trade receivables and how much is due from each of them. To rectify this, an account is held for each trade receivable in the sales ledger. This is in the form of a ledger account with the same debit and credit entries that are used in the general ledger. The big difference is that the sales ledger is a subsidiary ledger: there is no double entry taking place. The accounts in the sales ledger are not part of the double entry system of the general ledger but completely separate 'memorandum' accounts. They just give information. As a result, under 'details' we include the day book and document number rather than the name of the other side of the transaction.

The entries in the sales ledger for these three trade receivables would be as follows:

Sales ledger

A's account

Details	£	Details	£
SDB – 78346	400		

B's account

Details	£	Details	£
SDB – 78347	600		

C's account

Details	£	Details	£
SDB – 78348	500		

Now suppose that £300 is received from A and £250 from C, both via BACS. We will look at the entries for these receipts in the general ledger and in the sales ledger.

In the general ledger, money in means a debit to the Bank account and therefore a credit to the sales ledger control account. In the sales ledger the individual accounts will also be credited with the amounts received.

General ledger

Bank account

Details	£	Details	£
Sales ledger control	300		
Sales ledger control	250		

Sales ledger control account

Details	£	Details	£
Sales	400	Bank	300
Sales	600	Bank	250
Sales	500		

Sales ledger

A's account

Details	£	Details	£
SDB – 78346	400	Bank – BACS	300

B's account

Details	£	Details	£
SDB – 78347	600		

C's account

Details	£	Details	£
SDB – 78348	500	Bank – BACS	250

Task 5

A credit customer James Daniels buys goods from your business on credit for £1,000 including VAT and later pays £800 by cheque. Record these transactions in his account in the sales ledger.

James Daniels

Details	£	Details	£

HOW IT WORKS

The same principles apply when dealing with trade payables in the purchases ledger. The double entry for purchases on credit and money paid to trade payables takes place in the general ledger in the PURCHASES LEDGER CONTROL ACCOUNT, and then each individual trade payable account in the purchases ledger is also updated.

Suppose that our business has three credit suppliers, D, E and F.

The following transactions take place with these suppliers:

Purchases on credit	D – invoice 67532	£200
	E – invoice 736	£350
	F – invoice 24425	£100
Payments made	D – BACS	£100
	E – cheque	£250

These transactions must now be recorded in the general ledger and the purchases ledger.

General ledger

Purchases account

Details	£	Details	£
Purchases ledger control	200		
Purchases ledger control	350		
Purchases ledger control	100		

Purchases ledger control account

Details	£	Details	£
Bank	100	Purchases	200
Bank	250	Purchases	350
		Purchases	100

Bank account

Details	£	Details	£
		Purchases ledger control	100
		Purchases ledger control	250

Purchases ledger

D's account

Details	£	Details	£
CB – BACS	100	PDB – 67532	200

E's account

Details	£	Details	£
CB – cheque	250	PDB – 736	350

F's account

Details	£	Details	£
		PDB – 24425	100

CHAPTER OVERVIEW

- The principles behind double entry bookkeeping are that:

  - Every transaction has two effects on a business

  - The owner is a separate entity from the business itself

  - The accounting equation (assets minus liabilities equals capital) is always true

- The two effects of each transaction are recorded in ledger accounts with a debit entry in one account and a credit entry in another account

- If money is paid out of the business then the bank account is credited. Money coming into the business is debited to the bank account

- Increases in assets and expenses are recorded on the debit side of their accounts, decreases on the credit side

- Increases in liabilities and income are recorded on the credit side of their accounts, decreases on the debit side

- Money paid into the business by the owner is recorded on the credit side of a capital account, and money or goods taken out of the business by the owner are recorded on the debit side of a drawings account

- Balancing the ledger accounts enables the business to determine key business information such as the balance on the bank account, sales for a period and how much is owed to trade payables

- The general ledger is the complete set of ledger accounts of a business

- The sales ledger and purchases ledger are subsidiary ledgers (not part of the general ledger) which contain a ledger account for each individual trade receivable or trade payable. They do not form part of the double entry system

- In the general ledger the sales ledger control account and the purchases ledger control account only contain total figures in relation to trade receivables (for sales, sales returns, receipts and discounts allowed) and trade payables (for purchases, purchases returns, payments and discounts received)

Keywords

Double entry bookkeeping – a system of accounting where the two effects of each transaction are recorded

Separate entity concept – the owner of a business is a completely separate entity to the business itself

Accounting equation – assets minus liabilities equals capital

Dual effect – every transaction a business undertakes has two effects on the business

Assets – something that a business owns

Liabilities – something that a business owes

Capital – the amount owed by the business to its owner as a separate entity

Income – what the business earns when it makes sales of goods or services to other parties

Expenses – what the business spends to purchase goods or services for the company

Drawings – amounts taken out of the business by the owner

Ledger accounts – the accounts in which each transaction is recorded – there will be a ledger account for each type of transaction such as sales and purchases and for every type of asset and liability

General ledger – this is where the double entry takes place for all of the transactions of the business

Debit – the debit side of a ledger account is the left hand side

Credit – the credit side of a ledger account is the right hand side

Drawings – the money or goods that the owner takes out of the business

Non-current asset – an asset which is for long-term use in the business eg machinery

Discounts allowed ledger account – expense account which records settlement discounts deducted by credit customers

Balance brought down – in the ledger account the term used to describe the balancing figure that makes the column with the smaller figure total the larger figure

Balance carried down – used on the opposite side of the account, the balancing figure is described as the balance carried down

Capital expenditure – on assets used in the long term ie in more than one period (non-current assets)

Keywords cont'd

Capital income – from sales of assets used in the long term

Revenue expenditure – payments for day-to-day running costs and purchases, including wages and interest paid to the bank

Revenue income – receipts from sales and other short-term income such as interest from the bank, rent and commission

Sales return ledger account – used to record customer returns

Purchases returns ledger account – used to record return of goods to suppliers

Discounts received ledger account – ledger account which records settlement discount deducted by the business when making payments to credit suppliers

Subsidiary ledgers – the sales ledger and purchases ledger, which are memorandum ledgers that are not part of the general ledger, contain a ledger account for each individual trade receivable or trade payable. Not part of the double entry system

Sales ledger control account – a general ledger account for trade receivables, representing the total of all the accounts in the sales ledger

Purchases ledger control account – a general ledger account for trade payables, representing the total of all the accounts in the purchases ledger

TEST YOUR LEARNING

Test 1

Identify the general ledger accounts that are debited and credited for each of the following transactions.

	Debit	Credit
Money paid into the business by the owner		
Purchases on credit		
Purchases of machinery for use in the business, paid for by cheque		
Sales on credit		
Money taken out of the business by the owner		

Test 2

The following account is in the general ledger at the close of day on 30 June.

(a) Insert the balance carried down together with date and details.
(b) Insert the totals.
(c) Insert the balance brought down together with date and details.

Sales ledger control account

Date	Details	Amount £	Date	Details	Amount £
1/6	Balance b/d	1,209	28/6	Bank	3,287
30/6	Sales	6,298	30/6	Sales returns	786
	Total			Total	

Test 3

The following transactions all took place on 30 November and have been entered into the sales day book as shown below. No entries have yet been made into the ledger system.

Sales Day Book

Date 20XX	Details	Invoice number	Total £	VAT @ 20% £	Net £
30 Nov	Fries & Co	23907	2,136	356	1,780
30 Nov	Hussey Enterprises	23908	3,108	518	2,590
30 Nov	Todd Trading	23909	3,720	620	3,100
30 Nov	Milford Ltd	23910	2,592	432	2,160
	Totals		11,556	1,926	9,630

What will be the entries in the general ledger?

General ledger

Account name	Amount £	Debit ✓	Credit ✓	Details in account

Test 4

The following transactions all took place on 30 November and have been entered into the Purchases Day Book as shown below. No entries have yet been made into the ledger system.

Purchases Day Book

Date 20XX	Details	Invoice number	Total £	VAT @ 20% £	Net £
30 Nov	Lindell Co	24577	2,136	356	1,780
30 Nov	Harris Rugs	829	5,256	876	4,380
30 Nov	Kinshasa Music	10/235	2,796	466	2,330
30 Nov	Calnan Ltd	9836524	2,292	382	1,910
	Totals		12,480	2,080	10,400

What will be the entries in the general ledger?

General ledger

Account name	Amount £	Debit ✓	Credit ✓	Details in account

chapter 7:
DOUBLE ENTRY FOR SALES AND TRADE RECEIVABLES

---
chapter coverage 📖

In this chapter we look at entering details of credit and cash sales, sales returns and cash received into the accounting records. The topics covered are:

- ✍ The books of prime entry for sales and trade receivables
- ✍ The sales and general ledgers
- ✍ Posting the Sales and Sales Returns Day Book
- ✍ Posting receipts from the debit side of the Cash Book
- ✍ Posting discounts allowed from the debit side of the Cash Book
- ✍ Posting receipts from the debit side of the Petty Cash Book

BOOKS OF PRIME ENTRY AND THE LEDGERS

In Chapter 6 we looked at double entry bookkeeping in the general ledger and the sales and purchases ledgers for the transactions of a business. In those examples we entered each individual transaction directly into the ledger accounts, and using double entry principles this meant that each transaction was in fact entered twice in the general ledger.

In practice, this would be impractical and therefore a step is built into the process before the ledger account entries are made.

The first stage of the accounting process is to enter details of transaction documents into the BOOKS OF PRIME ENTRY, which we saw in Chapter 3.

TRANSACTION DOCUMENTS → BOOKS OF PRIME ENTRY → LEDGER ACCOUNTS

Three books of prime entry are relevant for sales and trade receivables:

- Invoices for a period are initially recorded in the Sales Day Book (SDB)

- Credit notes are recorded in the Sales Returns Day Book (SRDB)

- All receipts (including some that are not related to sales) and also discounts allowed are recorded in the debit side of the Cash Book (CB).

Both the general ledger and the sales ledger are affected by transactions involving sales and trade receivables, though it is only the general ledger that is part of the double entry system.

POSTING THE SALES DAY BOOK

The next stage of the accounting process is to transfer the details from the book of prime entry – we will look at the sales day book first – to the accounting records, in this case:

- The general ledger (so we will be **debiting trade receivables** and **crediting sales**), and

- The sales ledger (where we will just be debiting the individual customer ledger accounts – the sales ledger is **not** part of the double entry bookkeeping system)

It is common to refer to the process of transferring data into the ledgers as POSTING to the ledgers from the day books.

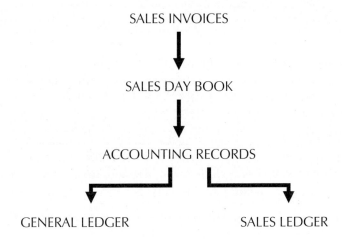

SALES INVOICES

SALES DAY BOOK

ACCOUNTING RECORDS

GENERAL LEDGER   SALES LEDGER

In order to do this the sales day book must first be totalled. This totalling process is also sometimes known as CASTING. The day book used before has now been totalled.

Date 20XX	Customer	Invoice number	Customer code	Invoice total £	VAT £	Net £
1 May	Grigsons Ltd	10356	SL 21	199.20	33.20	166.00
1 May	Hall & Co	10357	SL 05	105.60	17.60	88.00
1 May	Harris & Sons	10358	SL 17	120.00	20.00	100.00
2 May	Jaytry Ltd	10359	SL 22	309.60	51.60	258.00
	Totals			734.40	122.40	612.00

When casting a day book it is very easy to make errors in your additions. Therefore it is always advisable to CROSS CAST the day book as well. This means adding the net total to the VAT to ensure that it adds back to the total of the invoice totals – if it does not then an error has been made in the casting (£612.00 + £122.40 = £734.40).

Posting to the general ledger

Now we want to post the totals into the general ledger. Remember the general ledger is where the double entry takes place so let us consider the double entry required here.

The sales day book represents the sales on credit that have been made by the business so:

- **Invoice total** is the amount that the customer must pay to the business – the net total plus VAT. Therefore this is the amount of the trade receivable so the invoice total column total is a **debit** entry in the SALES LEDGER CONTROL ACCOUNT (SLCA) in the general ledger.

- **Net total** is the total of credit sales – the business makes no profit out of charging VAT as it is paid over to HM Revenue and Customs (HMRC), therefore the VAT is excluded from the sales total. This net total column total must be a **credit** entry in the ledger account for SALES.

- **VAT total** is the amount of VAT that is owed as a liability to HMRC and as such is a **credit** entry in the VAT ledger account.

General ledger

Sales ledger control account (SLCA)

Details	£	Details	£
Sales*	734.40		

Sales account

Details	£	Details	£
		SLCA	612.00

VAT account

Details	£	Details	£
		Sales*	122.40

While there are three different entries for these transactions, as always in double entry the total of the debit entries must equal the total of the credit entries:

Debit		£734.40
Credits	£612.00 + £122.40 =	£734.40

* Note that in general in the Details we include the name of the other account to be debited or credited. In the case of the sales ledger control account however the other side of the entry is split between two accounts, Sales and VAT. In this case we include the name of the primary or linking transaction, Sales, under Details in the SLCA. The same is true in the VAT account, where again we include the name of the linking transaction, Sales, under Details.

Task 1

Identify the general ledger accounts that the following totals from the Sales Day Book will be posted to and whether they are a debit or a credit entry:

	Account name	Debit	Credit
Invoice total			
VAT			
Net			

Posting to the sales ledger

So far we have completed the double entry in the general ledger for credit sales, but it is vitally important that we go on to post the invoice totals to the individual trade receivable accounts in the SALES LEDGER, which is the collection of ledger accounts for individual credit customers. It is not part of the double entry system and is known as a SUBSIDIARY LEDGER.

Step 1   Find the individual customer's account in the sales ledger using the customer code in the reference column of the Sales Day Book.

Step 2   Enter the invoice total of the invoice, including VAT, on the debit side of the customer's account.

You will remember that we completed the following entries for the four invoices in the Sales Day Book in the sales ledger accounts in Chapter 3. You can assume the invoice in the last ledger account, Sukie Ltd, was posted three days ago.

Sales ledger

Grigsons Ltd			SL 21
Details	£	Details	£
SDB – 10356	199.20		

Hall & Co			SL 05
Details	£	Details	£
SDB – 10357	105.60		

Harris & Sons			SL 17
Details	£	Details	£
SDB – 10358	120.00		

Jaytry Ltd			SL 22
Details	£	Details	£
SDB – 10359	309.60		

Sukie Ltd			SL 39
Details	£	Details	£
SDB – 10350	1,673.00		

Remember that in the sales ledger we use the details from the book of original entry (the invoice number from the SDB in this case) as this makes it easier to trace the source of the transaction.

A useful double check at this point is that the total of all the postings we made to the sales ledger (ignore the Sukie Ltd posting) is the same as the single debit posting to the sales ledger control account from the Sales Day Book:

	Debit entries £	
Grigsons Ltd	199.20	
Hall & Co	105.60	Sales ledger
Harris & Sons	120.00	
Jaytry Ltd	309.60	
Sales ledger control	734.40	General ledger

POSTING THE SALES RETURNS DAY BOOK

We have already considered the preparation of credit notes for valid and authorised sales returns, and their entry into the Sales Returns Day Book. Now we will look at posting the sales returns day book to the general and sales ledgers.

First of all it needs to be cast and the totals cross cast.

Date 20XX	Customer	Credit note number	Customer code	Credit note total £	VAT £	Net £
4 May	Grigsons Ltd	CN668	SL 21	72.00	12.00	60.00
5 May	Harris & Sons	CN669	SL 17	96.00	16.00	80.00
	Totals			168.00	28.00	140.00

Again, remember to check that the column totals do cross cast to the total of the credit note totals (£140.00 + £28.00 = £168.00).

In the general ledger the three column totals must be entered into the ledger accounts. The double entry is the reverse of that for a sale on credit, but let's consider the logic behind each entry:

- **Credit note total** As the customers have returned these goods they will no longer have to pay for them, so we must deduct the total column for the credit notes total. As trade receivables are decreased, this total is a **credit** entry in the sales ledger control account.

- **Net total** is the total of sales returns for the period which is effectively the reverse of a sale. Therefore a **debit** entry is required in the SALES RETURNS LEDGER ACCOUNT (not the sales account – we keep these separate).

- **VAT** As these returned goods have not been sold the VAT is no longer due to HMRC. Therefore a **debit** entry is made in the VAT account.

General ledger

Sales ledger control account

Details	£	Details	£
Sales	734.40	Sales returns	168.00

Sales returns account

Details	£	Details	£
SLCA	140.00		

VAT account

Details	£	Details	£
Sales returns	28.00	Sales	122.40

Again note that:

- the total of the two new debit entries is equal to the new credit entry: £140.00 + £28.00 = £168.00

- in both the SLCA and the VAT account we include the linking transaction 'Sales returns' under Details, while in the sales returns account we include 'SLCA'

Posting to the sales ledger

We have completed the double entry in the general ledger for sales returns from credit customers, so now we must enter each individual credit note in the relevant customer's account in the sales ledger. The amount to be used is the credit note total and the trade receivable's account must be credited with this figure to show that the customer no longer owes this amount.

Grigsons Ltd				SL 21
Details	£	Details		£
SDB – 10356	199.20	SRDB – CN668		72.00

Harris & Sons				SL 17
Details	£	Details		£
SDB – 103568	120.00	SRDB – CN669		96.00

Again a useful double check is that the total of all the postings to the sales ledger from the Sales Returns Day Book is the same as the single credit posting to the sales ledger control account:

	Credit entries £	
Grigsons Ltd	72.00	Sales ledger
Harris & Sons	96.00	
Sales ledger control	168.00	General ledger

Task 2

A credit note for £200 plus VAT has been issued to a customer. How much will be entered in the sales ledger control account in the general ledger and the customer's account in the sales ledger, and will these entries be debits or credits?

	Amount £	Debit ✓	Credit ✓
Sales ledger control account (general ledger)			
Customer's account (sales ledger)			

Posting an analysed Sales Day Book

Where an organisation analyses its sales into geographical area or product family, posting to the general ledger is the same except that there will be a posting to more than one sales account.

HOW IT WORKS

Analysed Sales Day Book

Date 20XX	Customer	Credit note number	Customer code	Invoice total £	VAT £	Net £	North £	South £	East £	West £
1/6	AB Ltd	936	SL23	120.00	20.00	100.00		100.00		
1/6	CD & Co	937	SL03	240.00	40.00	200.00			200.00	
2/6	EF Ltd	938	SL45	64.80	10.80	54.00	54.00			
3/6	GH Ltd	939	SL18	144.00	24.00	120.00				120.00
4/6	IJ Bros	940	SL25	72.00	12.00	60.00		60.00		
				640.80	106.80	534.00	54.00	160.00	200.00	120.00

The posting of this sales day book in the general ledger requires a separate sales account for each area as follows:

Sales ledger control account

Details	£	Details	£
Sales	640.80		

VAT account

Details	£	Details	£
		Sales	106.80

Sales account – North

Details	£	Details	£
		SLCA	54.00

Sales account – South

Details	£	Details	£
		SLCA	160.00

Sales account – East

Details	£	Details	£
		SLCA	200.00

Sales account – West

Details	£	Details	£
		SLCA	120.00

You can again check that all of the credit entries do add up to the total of the debit entry £(106.80 + 54.00 + 160.00 + 200.00 + 120.00 = 640.80).

The posting of the debit entries to the sales ledger are unaffected as it is the individual invoice totals that are posted to the sales ledger.

POSTING THE CASH BOOK

We looked briefly at the cash book in Chapter 3, where we saw that it is the book of prime entry for the initial recording of receipts of cash in the business's bank account. An example related to receipts of cash is shown here:

Date	Details	Ref	Bank £	VAT £	Discounts allowed £	Cash sales £	Sales ledger £	Sundry £
10 May	Grigsons Ltd	SL 21	127.20				127.20	
10 May	Sukie Ltd	SL 39	1,651.00		22.00		1,651.00	
10 May	Cash sale		360.00	60.00		300.00		
10 May	Capital introduced		1,000.00					1,000.00

This shows that:

- Two customers – Grigsons Ltd and Sukie Ltd – have respectively paid £127.20 and £1,651.00 to the business for the sales made to them on credit. In addition, Sukie Ltd has been allowed a settlement discount
- A cash sale has been made, so both the net sale and the VAT are recorded in the Cash Book
- The business's owner has introduced some additional capital.

As with the Sales Day Book, the Cash Book is posted to the general ledger. Some – but not all – transactions are also posted to the sales ledger.

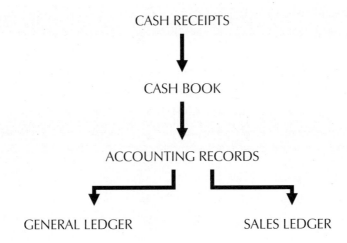

CASH RECEIPTS

CASH BOOK

ACCOUNTING RECORDS

GENERAL LEDGER   SALES LEDGER

In order to do this the Cash Book must first be cast.

Date	Details	Ref	Bank £	VAT £	Discounts allowed £	Cash sales £	Sales ledger £	Sundry £
10 May	Grigsons Ltd	SL 21	£127.20				127.20	
10 May	Sukie Ltd	SL 39	1,651.00		22.00		1,651.00	
10 May	Cash sale		360.00	60.00		300.00		
10 May	Capital introduced		1,000.00					1,000.00
	Totals		3,138.20	60.00	22.00	300.00	1,778.20	1,000.00

You will see straightaway that the Cash Book does **not** cross-cast to the bank total: £(60.00 + 22.00 + 300.00 + 1,778.20 + 1,000.00) = £3,160.20. The difference is £(3,160.20 – 3,138.20) = £22.00. This is the amount of the settlement discounts allowed, which is not received as cash so it is not included in the total cash receipt from Sukie Ltd shown in the 'bank' column.

Posting to the general ledger

All the other totals in the Cash Book are posted either to the debit or the credit side of an account in the general ledger, but the settlement discounts allowed total is posted twice:

- The debit entry is to the discounts allowed expense account
- The credit entry is to the sales ledger control account

Posting the Cash Book is therefore a more complicated task than posting the Sales Day Book.

BPP
LEARNING MEDIA

HOW IT WORKS

The easiest way to see how the postings are made in the general ledger is to show the relevant general ledger account name beneath each Cash Book total, with an indication of whether the posting is a debit entry or a credit entry:

Date	Details	Ref	Bank £	VAT £	Discount allowed £	Cash sales £	Sales ledger £	Sundry £
	Totals		3,138.20	60.00	22.00	300.00	1,778.20	1,000.00
General ledger account	Debit entry		Bank		Discounts allowed			
	Credit entry			VAT	Sales ledger control	Sales	Sales ledger control	Capital

We can now make the postings to the general ledger. Note that for the debit entry in the Bank account we have included 'Bank receipts' under Details. Unlike with the Sales and Sales Returns Day Books, there are more than two other accounts which receive the other side of this entry (ie Sales and Capital), and the transactions are not linked. For the sake of neatness therefore we have used the catch-all 'Bank receipts' as a narrative here.

General ledger

Bank account

Details	£	Details	£
Bank receipts	3,138.20		

Sales ledger control account

Details	£	Details	£
Sales	734.40	Sales returns	168.00
		Bank (cash)	1,778.20
		Bank (discounts allowed)	22.00

Sales account

Details	£	Details	£
		SLCA	612.00
		Bank	300.00

Sales returns account

Details	£	Details	£
SLCA	140.00		

VAT account

Details	£	Details	£
Sales returns	28.00	Sales	122.40
		Bank	60.00

Discounts allowed account

Details	£	Details	£
Bank (SLCA)	22.00		

Capital account

Details	£	Details	£
		Bank	1,000.00

A useful double check is that the debit and credit postings marked 'Bank' in the ledger accounts balance each other out (although you should note that usually the discounts allowed posting would not be marked Bank but would instead just contain the details of the two opposing accounts, Discounts allowed and SLCA):

Ledger account	Debit entries £	Credit entries £
Bank	3,138.20	
Sales ledger control		1,778.20
Sales ledger control		22.00
Sales		300.00
VAT		60.00
Discounts allowed	22.00	
Capital		1,000.00
	3,160.20	3,160.20

Posting to the sales ledger

We also need to enter each sales-related receipt and the settlement discount in the customers' accounts in the sales ledger. The amount for the receipt of cash is the amount in the 'sales ledger' column and this must be entered in the **credit** side of the ledger account as it is a reduction in how much the customer owes us. The amount for settlement discount allowed is the amount in the discounts allowed column and again must be entered on the **credit** side of the customer's account as it reduces the amount owed.

Remember that no debit entries are made as the sales ledger is not part of the double entry system. In addition, we do not post all the receipts in the cash book to the sales ledger: the two cash sales amounts (for the net sale and the related VAT) and the capital receipt are **not** posted to the sales ledger.

Sales ledger

Grigsons Ltd   SL 21

Details	£	Details	£
SDB – 10356	199.20	SRDB – CN668	72.00
		CB – cash	127.20

Sukie Ltd   SL 39

Details	£	Details	£
SDB – 10350	1,673.00	CB – cash	1,651.00
		CB – discounts allowed	22.00

Task 3

You have been handed the sales and sales returns day books and the debit side of the Cash Book for Mr Chapter, plus relevant ledger accounts from his general and sales ledgers.

Total each day book, and then post each one to the ledgers.

Sales Day Book

Customer	Invoice number	Customer code	Invoice total £	VAT £	Net £
Trissom Ltd	124	SL 09	1,190.00	190.00	1,000.00
Miley & Co	125	SL 22	540.00	90.00	450.00
Totals					

Sales Returns Day Book

Customer	Credit note number	Customer code	Credit note total £	VAT £	Net £
Trissom Ltd	07	SL 09	238.00	38.00	200.00
Miley & Co	08	SL 22	36.00	6.00	30.00
Totals					

Cash Book

Details	Ref	Bank £	VAT £	Discounts allowed £	Cash sales £	Sales ledger £	Other £
Trissom Ltd	SL 09	912.00		40.00		912.00	
Miley & Co	SL 22	504.00				504.00	
Cash sale		240.00	40.00		200.00		
Totals							

General ledger

Bank account

Details	£	Details	£

Sales ledger control account

Details	£	Details	£

Sales account

Details	£	Details	£

Sales returns account

Details	£	Details	£

VAT account

Details	£	Details	£

Discounts allowed account

Details	£	Details	£

Sales ledger

Trissom Ltd · SL 09

Details	£	Details	£

Miley & Co · SL 22

Details	£	Details	£

The Cash Book as part of the general ledger

The Cash Book is a book of prime entry that records cash coming into and going out of the business's bank account. We have seen so far that, in relation to receipts, this means postings from it are always to the debit side of the Bank ledger account in the general ledger, with credit entries being posted to the sales ledger control account, sales, VAT etc.

In many businesses, the Cash Book is treated as **both** a book of prime entry **and** as part of the general ledger. This means that for receipts the Cash Book is itself the debit side of the Bank general ledger account (we shall see that the credit side of the account is the Cash Book where payments are recorded). The effect of this is that:

- There is no need to post a debit entry for the total receipts from the Cash Book shown in the Bank column

- There is no Bank general ledger account

- Credit entries, and both entries in respect of discounts allowed, are posted from the Cash Book as usual

Task 4

The Cash Book for a business acts as both a book of prime entry and as part of the general ledger. Total receipts for the last month are as follows:

Details	Bank £	VAT £	Discounts allowed £	Cash sales £	Sales ledger £
Totals	5,236.50	20.00	65.00	100.00	5,116.50

What entries will be posted to the general ledger (tick debit or credit for each entry)?

Account name	Amount £	Debit ✓	Credit ✓

POSTING THE PETTY CASH BOOK

We looked briefly at the Petty Cash Book in Chapter 3, where we saw that in relation to receipts of petty cash it is the book of prime entry for the initial recording of receipts of cash from the business's bank account into the petty cash box. An example is shown here:

Date	Details	Total £
10 May	Cash	150.00

This simply shows that the business has placed £150 in notes and coin in the petty cash box.

Receipts into the Petty Cash Book are posted only to the general ledger, not to the sales ledger.

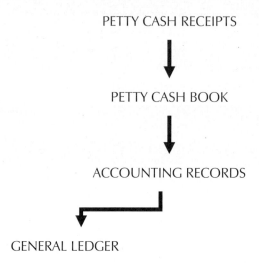

PETTY CASH RECEIPTS

PETTY CASH BOOK

ACCOUNTING RECORDS

GENERAL LEDGER

HOW IT WORKS

As there are so few receipts into petty cash the Petty Cash Book rarely needs casting and cross casting. Instead it is posted straight to the general ledger.

The receipt of cash into the petty cash box is actually an internal transfer between the Bank ledger account and the petty cash ledger account (sometimes called the petty cash control account).

- The **debit** side of the transaction is posted from the Petty Cash Book to the petty cash account in the general ledger

Petty cash account

Details	£	Details	£
Bank	150.00		

- The **credit** side of the transaction is included in the posting from the Cash Book in relation to payments to the Bank ledger account – as we shall see in Chapter 8.

The Petty Cash Book as part of the general ledger

As with the main Cash Book, in many businesses the Petty Cash Book is treated as **both** a book of prime entry **and** as part of the general ledger. This means that for receipts the Petty Cash Book is itself the debit side of a general ledger account (we shall see in Chapter 8 that for payments from petty cash the Petty Cash Book can itself act as the credit side of a general ledger account). The effect of this is that:

- There is no need to post a debit entry for the total receipts column from the Petty Cash Book

- There is no petty cash general ledger account

CHAPTER OVERVIEW

- The first stage of the accounting process is to enter details of transactions into the books of prime entry eg Sales and Sales Returns Day Books and Cash Book

- The second stage of the accounting process is to transfer details from the books of prime entry to the accounting records ie the general ledger and sales ledger

- The Sales Day Book must be totalled and the totals entered into the ledger accounts in the general ledger

- Each individual sales invoice must also be entered into the individual trade receivable's account in the sales ledger

- The Sales Returns Day Book must also be totalled and posted to the general ledger and the sales ledger

- The Cash Book must be totalled and posted to the general ledger

- Each cash receipt in the sales ledger column of the Cash Book must also be entered into the individual trade receivable's account in the sales ledger

- The discounts allowed column in the Cash Book must have both a debit and a credit posting in the general ledger, and each individual entry must be credited to a trade receivable's account in the sales ledger

- The Petty Cash Book must be totalled and posted to petty cash (or petty cash control) account in the general ledger

Keywords

Posting – transferring data from the books of prime entry (day books) into the ledgers

Casting – an accounting term for adding up a column of figures

Cross cast – adding up the totals of a number of columns to check that they add back to the overall total

Sales ledger control account – a general ledger account for trade receivables, representing the total of all the accounts in the sales ledger

Subsidiary ledgers – ledgers that are not part of the general ledger and which contain a ledger account for each individual trade receivable or trade payable. Not part of the double entry system

Sales returns ledger account – used to record customer returns

TEST YOUR LEARNING

Test 1

From the Sales Day Book and Sales Returns Day book below, make the relevant entries in the general ledger and sales ledger accounts.

Sales Day Book

Date	Customer	Invoice number	Customer code	Invoice total £	VAT £	Net £
21/9	Dagwell Enterprises	56401	SL15	948.60	158.10	790.50
21/9	G Thomas & Co	56402	SL30	3,537.60	589.60	2,948.00
21/9	Polygon Stores	56403	SL03	1,965.60	327.60	1,638.00
21/9	Weller Enterprises	56404	SL18	1,152.00	192.00	960.00
				7,603.80	1,267.30	6,336.50

Sales Returns Day Book

Date	Customer	Credit note number	Customer code	Credit note total £	VAT £	Net £
21/9	Whitehill Superstores	08650	SL37	356.40	59.40	297.00
23/9	Dagwell Enterprises	08651	SL15	244.80	40.80	204.00
				601.20	100.20	501.00

General ledger

Sales ledger control account

Details	£	Details	£

Sales account

Details	£	Details	£

Sales returns account

Details	£	Details	£

VAT account

Details	£	Details	£

Sales ledger

Dagwell Enterprises   SL 15

Details	£	Details	£

G Thomas & Co   SL 30

Details	£	Details	£

Polygon Stores   SL 03

Details	£	Details	£

Weller Enterprises   SL 18

Details	£	Details	£

Whitehill Superstores   SL 37

Details	£	Details	£

Test 2

Post the Cash Book below to the general ledger and sales ledger. Note the Cash Book is itself part of the general ledger.

Cash Book

Date	Details	Ref	Total £	VAT £	Discounts allowed £	Cash sales £	Sales ledger £
				£	£	£	£
30/6	Cash sales		372.00	62.00		310.00	
30/6	H Henry	SL0115	146.79				146.79
30/6	P Peters	SL0135	221.55		6.85		221.55
30/6	K Kilpin	SL0128	440.30				440.30
30/6	Cash sales		300.76	50.12		250.64	
30/6	B Bennet	SL0134	57.80				57.80
30/6	S Shahir	SL0106	114.68		3.55		114.68
			1,653.88	112.12	10.40	560.64	981.12

General ledger

VAT account   GL 562

Details	£	Details	£

Sales account   GL 049

Details	£	Details	£

Sales ledger control account   GL 827

Details	£	Details	£

Discounts allowed account   GL 235

Details	£	Details	£

Sales ledger

H Henry   **SL 0115**

Details	£	Details	£

P Peters   **SL 0135**

Details	£	Details	£

K Kilpin   **SL 0128**

Details	£	Details	£

B Bennet   **SL 0134**

Details	£	Details	£

S Shahir   **SL 0106**

Details	£	Details	£

Test 3

Post the Cash Book below to the general ledger and sales ledger. The cash book is **not** part of the general ledger.

Cash Book

Date	Details	Ref	Total £	VAT £	Discounts allowed £	Cash sales £	Sales ledger £
20/5	G Gonpipe	SL55	332.67				332.6
20/5	Cash sales		672.00	112.00		560.00	
20/5	J Jimmings	SL04	127.37		6.70		127.3
20/5	N Nutely	SL16	336.28		17.70		336.28
20/5	T Turner	SL21	158.35				158.3
20/5	Cash sales		336.90	56.15		280.75	
20/5	R Ritner	SL45	739.10		38.90		739.10
			2,702.67	168.15	63.30	840.75	1,693.7

General ledger codes

Bank	100
Sales	110
Discounts allowed	280
Sales ledger control	560
VAT	710

General ledger

Bank   **GL 100**

Details	£	Details	£

VAT account   **GL 710**

Details	£	Details	£

Sales account   **GL 110**

Details	£	Details	£

Sales ledger control account   **GL 560**

Details	£	Details	£

Discounts allowed account   **GL 280**

Details	£	Details	£

Sales ledger

G Gonpipe   **SL 55**

Details	£	Details	£

J Jimmings   **SL 04**

Details	£	Details	£

N Nutely   SL 16

Details	£	Details	£

T Turner   SL 21

Details	£	Details	£

R Ritner   SL 45

Details	£	Details	£

Test 4

The following transactions all took place on 30 November and have been entered into the Sales Day Book as shown below. No entries have yet been made into the ledger system.

Sales Day Book

Date 20XX	Details	Invoice number	Total £	VAT @ 20% £	Net £
30 Nov	Fries & Co	23907	2,136	356	1,780
30 Nov	Hussey Enterprises	23908	3,108	518	2,590
30 Nov	Todd Trading	23909	3,720	620	3,100
30 Nov	Milford Ltd	23910	2,592	432	2,160
	Totals		11,556	1,926	9,630

Make the required entries in the general ledger.

VAT account

Details	£	Details	£

Sales account

Details	£	Details	£

Sales ledger control account

Details	£	Details	£

chapter 8:
DOUBLE ENTRY FOR PURCHASES AND TRADE PAYABLES

---

chapter coverage 📖

In this chapter we look at entering details of credit and cash purchases, purchases returns and cash paid into the accounting records. The topics covered are:

- ✍ The books of prime entry for purchases and trade payables
- ✍ The purchases and general ledgers
- ✍ Posting the Purchases and Purchases Returns Day Books
- ✍ Posting payments from the credit side of the Cash Book
- ✍ Posting discounts received from the credit side of the Cash Book
- ✍ The Petty Cash Book
- ✍ Posting payments from the credit side of the Petty Cash Book

BOOKS OF PRIME ENTRY AND THE LEDGERS

As with sales and trade receivables, the first stage of the accounting process for purchases and trade payables is to enter details of transaction documents into the relevant books of prime entry:

TRANSACTION ➡ BOOKS OF ➡ LEDGER
DOCUMENTS   PRIME ENTRY   ACCOUNTS

Three books of prime entry are relevant for purchases and trade payables:

- Purchase invoices received in a period are initially recorded in the Purchases Day Book
- Credit notes received are recorded in the Purchases Returns Day Book
- All payments (including some that are not related to purchases) plus settlement discounts received from suppliers are recorded in the Cash Book

Both the general ledger and the purchases ledger are affected by transactions involving purchases and trade payables, though it is only the general ledger that is part of the double entry system.

POSTING THE PURCHASES DAY BOOK

The next stage of the accounting process is to transfer details from the books of prime entry to the accounting records. We will look at the Purchases Day Book first.

The Purchases Day Book needs to be posted to:

- The general ledger (so we will be **crediting trade payables** and **debiting purchases** or some other **expense**)
- The purchases ledger (where we will just be crediting the individual supplier ledger accounts – the purchases ledger is **not** part of the double entry bookkeeping system)

PURCHASE INVOICES

⬇

PURCHASES DAY BOOK

⬇

ACCOUNTING RECORDS

GENERAL LEDGER   PURCHASES LEDGER

BPP
LEARNING MEDIA

HOW IT WORKS

As with sales, we must first cast and cross cast the Purchases Day Book.

Date 20XX	Supplier	Invoice number	Supplier code	Invoice total £	VAT £	Purchases £	Telephone £	Stationery £
1 May	Haley Ltd	33728	PL 25	60.00	10.00			50.00
1 May	JJ Bros	242G	PL 14	1,440.00	240.00	1,200.00		
1 May	B Tel	530624	PL 06	156.00	26.00		130.00	
1 May	Shipley & Co	673	PL 59	4,800.00	800.00	4,000.00		
	Totals			6,456.00	1,076.00	5,200.00	130.00	50.00

The total of the analysis columns – in this case, for purchases, telephone and stationery – plus the VAT must add back to the total of the invoice totals – if not then an error has been made in the casting: £(5,200.00 + 130.00 + 50.00 + 1,076.00) = £6,456.00.

Posting to the general ledger

Now we want to post the totals into the general ledger. The Purchases Day Book represents the purchases on credit that have been made by the business so:

- **Invoice total** is the amount that the business must pay to the supplier – the net total plus VAT. Therefore this is the amount of the payable, so the invoice total column total is a **credit** entry in the trade payables account in the general ledger. This is usually known as the PURCHASES LEDGER CONTROL ACCOUNT (PLCA).

- The **VAT total** is the amount of VAT that is reclaimable from HMRC (ie it is an asset) and as such is a **debit** entry in the VAT ledger account.

- The **purchases**, **telephone** and **stationery** totals are the cost to the business of the goods it has acquired and the expenses it has incurred – the business does not suffer VAT as a cost as it is paid back by HM Revenue and Customs, so VAT is excluded from the purchases and expenses totals. The totals in these columns must be **debit** entries in the relevant general ledger accounts.

General ledger

Purchases ledger control account

Details	£	Details	£
		Purchases*	6,456.00

* Several accounts (purchases, telephone and stationery) take the other side of this entry. For the sake of neatness we have just included one under Details, namely Purchases.

Purchases account

Details	£	Details	£
PLCA	5,200.00		

Telephone account

Details	£	Details	£
PLCA	130.00		

Stationery account

Details	£	Details	£
PLCA	50.00		

VAT account

Details	£	Details	£
Purchases	1,076.00		

Under Details in the VAT account we include the linking transaction of Purchases, as we saw in Chapter 7.

While there are five different entries for these transactions, as always in double entry the total of the debit entries must equal the total of the credit entries:

Debit   £(5,200.00 + 130.00 + 50.00 + 1,076.00) £6,456.00

Credits   £6,456.00

Task 1

Identify the general ledger accounts that the following totals from the Purchases Day Book will be posted to, and whether they are a debit or a credit entry:

	Account name	Debit	Credit
Invoice total			
VAT			
Purchases			

Posting to the purchases ledger

We have completed the double entry in the general ledger for credit purchases, so we now need to post the invoice totals to the individual payable accounts in the PURCHASES LEDGER, which is the collection of ledger accounts for individual credit suppliers. It is not part of the double entry system and, like the sales ledger, is known as a subsidiary ledger.

Step 1   Find the individual supplier's account in the purchases ledger using the supplier code.

Step 2   Enter the invoice total of the invoice (ie including VAT) on the credit side of the supplier's account.

Purchases ledger

			Haley Ltd		PL 25
Details		£	Details		£
			PDB – 33728		60.00

			JJ Bros		PL 14
Details		£	Details		£
			PDB – 242G		1,440.00

			B Tel		PL 06
Details		£	Details		£
			PDB – 530824		156.00

			Shipley & Co		PL 59
Details		£	Details		£
			PDB – 673		4,800.00

A useful double check at this point is that the total of all the postings we have just made to the purchases ledger is the same as the single credit posting to the purchases ledger control account from the Purchases Day Book:

	Credit entries £	
Haley Ltd	60.00	
JJ Bros	1,440.00	Purchases ledger
B Tel	156.00	
Shipley & Co	4,800.00	
Purchases ledger control	6,456.00	General ledger

POSTING THE PURCHASES RETURNS DAY BOOK

We have already considered the preparation of credit notes for valid and authorised purchases returns, and their entry into the Purchases Returns Day Book. Now we will look at posting the Purchases Returns Day Book to the general and purchases ledgers.

HOW IT WORKS

First of all, it needs to be cast and the totals cross cast.

Date 20XX	Supplier	Credit note number	Supplier code	Credit note total £	VAT £	Purchases £	Telephone £	Stationery £
4 May	Haley Ltd	CN783	PL25	24.00	4.00			20.00
5 May	JJ Bros	C52246	PL14	69.60	11.60	58.00		
				93.60	15.60	58.00		20.00

Again remember to check that the column totals do cross cast to the total of the credit note totals (£20.00 + £58.00 + 15.60 = £93.60).

Posting to the general ledger

In the general ledger the column totals must be entered into the ledger accounts. The double entry is the reverse of that for a purchase on credit, but let's consider the logic behind each entry:

- **Credit note total** – As the business has returned these goods to suppliers it will no longer have to pay for them, so we must deduct the total column for the credit note totals. As trade payables are decreased, this total is a **debit** entry in the purchases ledger control account.

- **VAT total** – As the cost of these returned goods has not been incurred the VAT is no longer reclaimable from HMRC. Therefore a **credit** entry is made in the VAT account.

The **purchases** and **stationery** totals are the reduction in the cost to the business of the goods it has returned – again VAT is excluded.

- The total in the purchases column is a **credit** entry in the purchases returns account.

- The total in the stationery column is a **credit** entry in the stationery returns account.

General ledger

Purchases ledger control account

Details	£	Details	£
Puchases returns*	93.60	Purchases	6,456.00

* Again for the sake of neatness we have included just one named linked account here even though there are two (stationery returns as well as purchases returns) plus VAT that take the other side of the entry.

Purchases returns account

Details	£	Details	£
		PLCA	58.00

Stationery returns account

Details	£	Details	£
		PLCA	20.00

VAT account

Details	£	Details	£
Purchases	1,076.00	Purchases returns	15.60

Again, note that the total of the three credit postings is equal to the debit posting: £58.00 + £20.00 + £15.60= £93.60.

Posting to the purchases ledger

We have completed the double entry in the general ledger for purchases returns to credit suppliers, so now we must enter each individual credit note in the supplier's account in the purchases ledger. The amount to be used is the credit note total and the trade payable's account must be **debited** with this figure to show that the business no longer owes the supplier this amount.

Purchases ledger

Haley Ltd — PL 25

Details	£	Details	£
PRDB – CN783	24.00	PDB – 33728	60.00

JJ Bros — PL 14

Details	£	Details	£
PRDB – C52246	69.60	PDB – 242G	1,440.00

Again, a useful double check is that the total of all the postings to the purchases ledger from the Purchases Returns Day Book is the same as the single debit posting to the purchases ledger control account.

	Debit entries £	
Haley Ltd	24.00	Purchases ledger
JJ Bros	69.60	
Purchases ledger control	93.60	General ledger

Task 2

A credit note for £600 plus VAT has been received from a supplier. How much will be entered in the purchases ledger control account in the general ledger and the supplier's account in the purchases ledger, and will this entry be a debit or a credit?

	Amount £	Debit	Credit
Purchases ledger control account (general ledger)			
Supplier's account (purchases ledger)			

POSTING THE CASH BOOK

We looked briefly at the Cash Book in Chapter 3, where we saw that it is the book of prime entry for the initial recording of payments of cash from the business's bank account. An example is shown here:

Date	Details	Ref	Bank £	VAT £	Discounts received £	Cash purchases £	Purchases ledger £	Petty cash £	Sundr £
10 May	Haley Ltd	PL 25	36.00				36.00		
10 May	Shipley & Co	PL 59	4,600.00		200.00		4,600.00		
10 May	Cash purchase		204.00	34.00		170.00			
10 May	Drawings		300.00						300.0(
10 May	Petty cash		150.00					150.00	

This shows that:

- The business has paid two suppliers – Haley Ltd and Shipley & Co – respectively £36.00 and £4,600.00 for the purchases made by it on credit. In addition, the business has taken up the offer of £200 settlement discount from Shipley & Co

- A cash purchase has been made, so both the purchase and the VAT are recorded in the cash book

- The business's owner has taken £300 in drawings for living expenses

- A cheque for £150 drawn on the business's bank account has been cashed as notes and coin, to be placed in the business's petty cash box

As with the Purchases Day Book, the Cash Book is posted to the general ledger. Some – but not all – transactions are also posted to the purchases ledger.

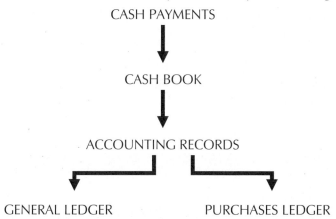

HOW IT WORKS

In order to post payments from the Cash Book to the ledgers it must first be cast and cross cast.

Date	Details	Ref	Bank £	VAT £	Discounts received £	Cash purchases £	Purchases ledger £	Petty cash £	Sundry £
10 May	Haley Ltd	PL 25	36.00				36.00		
10 May	Shipley & Co	PL 59	4,600.00		200.00		4,600.00		
10 May	Cash purchase		204.00	34.00		170.00			
10 May	Drawings		300.00						300.00
10 May	Petty cash		150.00					150.00	
	Totals		5,290.00	34.00	200.00	170.00	4,636.00	150.00	300.00

You will see straightaway that the Cash Book does **not** cross cast to the bank total: £(34.00 + 200.00 + 170.00 + 4,636.00 + 150.00 + 300.00) = £5,490.00. The difference is £(5,490.00 – 5,290.00) = £200.00. As we would expect having seen how the cash book for receipts operated in Chapter 7, this is the amount of the settlement discount which has been received from the supplier. It is not paid as cash so it is not included in the total cash payment to Shipley & Co shown in the 'Bank' column.

Posting to the general ledger

All the other totals in the Cash Book are posted either to the debit or the credit side of an account in the general ledger, but the settlement discounts received total is posted twice:

- The debit entry is to the purchases ledger control account

- The credit entry is to the discounts received account, which is a type of income account

Posting the Cash Book is therefore a slightly more complicated task than posting the Purchases Day Book.

HOW IT WORKS

The easiest way to see how the postings are made in the general ledger is to show the relevant general ledger account name beneath each Cash Book total, with an indication of whether the posting is a debit entry or a credit entry:

Date	Details	Bank £	VAT £	Discounts received £	Cash purchases £	Purchases ledger £	Petty cash £	Sundr £
	Totals	5,290.00	34.00	200.00	170.00	4,636.00	150.00	300.0
General ledger account	Debit entry		VAT	Purchases ledger control	Purchases	Purchases ledger control	Petty cash	Drawin
	Credit entry	Bank		Discounts received				

We can then make the postings to the general ledger:

General ledger

Bank account

Details	£	Details	£
		Bank payments*	5,290.00

*As in Chapter 7, because there are a number of unlinked accounts which take the opposing entries, we have used a catch-all narrative under Details here (Bank payments).

Purchases ledger control account

Details	£	Details	£
Purchases returns	93.60	Purchases	6,456.00
Bank	4,636.00		
Discounts received	200.00		

Purchases account

Details	£	Details	£
PLCA	5,200.00		
Bank	170.00		

Purchases returns account

Details	£	Details	£
		PLCA	58.00

Telephone account

Details	£	Details	£
PLCA	130.00		

Stationery account

Details	£	Details	£
PLCA	50.00		

Stationery returns account

Details	£	Details	£
		PLCA	20.00

VAT account

Details	£	Details	£
Purchases	1,076.00	Purchases returns	15.60
Bank	34.00		

Discounts received account

Details	£	Details	£
		PLCA	200.00

Petty cash account

Details	£	Details	£
Bank	150.00		

Drawings account

Details	£	Details	£
Bank	300.00		

A useful double check is that the most recent debit and credit postings in the ledger accounts balance each other out:

Ledger account	Debit entries £	Credit entries £
Bank		5,290.00
Purchases ledger control (cash)	4,636.00	
Purchases ledger control (discounts received)	200.00	
Purchases	170.00	
VAT	34.00	
Discounts received		200.00
Petty cash	150.00	
Drawings	300.00	
	5,490.00	5,490.00

Posting to the purchases ledger

We also need to enter each purchases-related payment and the settlement discount in the suppliers' accounts in the purchases ledger. The amount for the payment of cash is the amount in the 'purchases ledger' column and this must be entered in the **debit** side of the ledger account as it is a reduction in how much the business owes. The amount for settlement discount received is the amount from the discounts received column in the Cash Book and again must be entered on the **debit** side of the supplier's account as it reduces the amount owed.

Remember that no credit entries are made as the purchases ledger is not part of the double entry system. In addition, we do not post the two cash purchases amounts (for the net purchase and the related VAT) nor the drawings payment to the purchases ledger.

Purchases ledger

Haley Ltd   **PL 25**

Details	£	Details	£
PRDB – CN783	24.00	PDB – 33728	60.00
CB	36.00		

Shipley & Co   **PL 59**

Details	£	Details	£
CB – cash	4,600.00	PDB – 673	4,800.00
CB – discount	200.00		

Task 3

You have been handed the unanalysed Purchases and Purchases Returns Day Books and the credit side of the Cash Book for Mr Chapter, plus relevant ledger accounts from his general and purchases ledgers.

Total each day book and then post each one to the ledgers.

Purchases Day Book

Supplier	Invoice number	Supplier code	Invoice total £	VAT £	Net £
Rawley Ltd	7869	PL 54	3,000.00	500.00	2,500.00
Jipsum plc	323980	PL 02	3,808.00	608.00	3,200.00
Totals					

Purchases Returns Day Book

Supplier	Credit note number	Supplier code	Credit note total £	VAT £	Net £
Rawley Ltd	CN627	PL 54	96.00	16.00	80.00
Jipsum plc	CN08	PL 02	476.00	76.00	400.00
Totals					

Purchases Returns Day Book

Cash Book

Details	Ref	Bank £	VAT £	Discounts received £	Cash purchases £	Purchases ledger £
Rawley Ltd	PL 54	2,904.00				2,904.00
Jipsum plc	PL 02	3,192.00		140.00		3,192.00
Cash purchase		720.00	120.00		600.00	
Totals						

General ledger

Bank account

Details	£	Details	£

Purchases ledger control account

Details	£	Details	£

Purchases account

Details	£	Details	£

Purchases returns account

Details	£	Details	£

VAT account

Details	£	Details	£

Discounts received account

Details	£	Details	£

Purchases ledger

Rawley Ltd   PL 54

Details	£	Details	£

Jipsum plc			PL 02
Details	**£**	**Details**	**£**

The Cash Book as part of the general ledger

The Cash Book for payments is a book of prime entry that records cash going out of the business's bank account. We have seen so far that this means postings from it are always to the credit side of the Bank ledger account in the general ledger, with debit entries being posted to the purchases ledger control account, purchases, VAT etc.

As we have seen already, in many businesses the Cash Book is treated as **both** a book of prime entry **and** part of the general ledger. This means that the Cash Book for payments is itself the credit side of a general ledger account (just as we saw in Chapter 7 that the debit side of the account is the Cash Book for receipts). The effect of this is that:

- There is no need to post a credit entry for the total column from the Cash Book

- There is no Bank general ledger account

- Debit entries from the Cash Book, plus both entries for discounts received, are posted as usual

Task 4

The Cash Book for a business is both a book of prime entry and part of the general ledger. Total payments for the last month are as follows:

Details	Bank £	VAT £	Discounts received £	Cash purchases £	Purchases ledger £
Totals	3,297.65	48.00	109.00	240.00	3,009.65

What entries will be posted to the general ledger (tick debit or credit for each entry)?

Account name	Amount £	Debit ✓	Credit ✓

POSTING THE PETTY CASH BOOK

We looked briefly at the Petty Cash Book in Chapter 3, where we saw that it is the book of prime entry for the initial recording of payments of cash from the business's petty cash. An example is shown here:

Date	Details	Voucher number	Total cash £	VAT £	Travel £	Postage £	Stationery £	Office cleaning £
10 May	Stationery – Lara Moschetta	067	48.00	8.00			40.00	
10 May	Post office – stamps	068	15.00			15.00		
10 May	Green Clean – window cleaning	069	30.00					30.00

This shows that:

- The business has reimbursed one employee, Lara Moschetta, for £48.00 of expenditure on stationery that Lara paid herself. Both the net amount and the VAT are recorded in the Petty Cash Book

- Money has been taken out of the petty cash box to make a purchase of postage stamps at the Post Office (no VAT)

- Money has also been taken out of the petty cash box to pay the business's window cleaner (no VAT)

The Petty Cash Book is posted only to the general ledger, not to the purchases ledger.

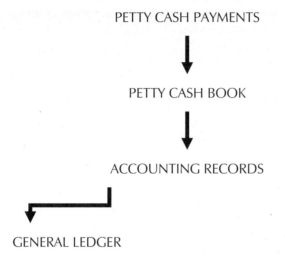

PETTY CASH PAYMENTS

PETTY CASH BOOK

ACCOUNTING RECORDS

GENERAL LEDGER

HOW IT WORKS

In order to do this the Petty Cash Book must first be cast and cross cast.

Date	Details	Voucher number	Total cash £	VAT £	Travel £	Postage £	Stationery £	Other £
10 May	Stationery – Lara Moschetta	067	48.00	8.00			40.00	
10 May	Post office – stamps	068	15.00			15.00		
10 May	Green Clean – window cleaning	069	30.00					30.00
	Totals		93.00	8.00		15.00	40.00	30.00

Posting to the general ledger

All the totals in the Petty Cash Book are posted either to the debit or the credit side of an account in the general ledger that bears the same name as the analysis column in the Petty Cash Book from which the posting is made.

HOW IT WORKS

The easiest way to see how the postings are made in the general ledger is to show the relevant general ledger account name beneath each Petty Cash Book total, with an indication of whether the posting is a debit entry or a credit entry:

Date	Details	Voucher number	Total cash £	VAT £	Travel £	Postage £	Stationery £	Office cleaning £
	Totals		93.00	8.00		15.00	40.00	30.00
	General ledger	Debit entry		VAT		Postage	Stationery	Office cleaning
		Credit entry	Petty cash					

Note that the petty cash account is the one that we updated in Chapter 7 with the receipt of £150 cash from the Bank account. It may also be called the petty cash control account.

We can now make the postings to the general ledger:

General ledger

Petty cash account

Details	£	Details	£
Bank	150.00	Petty cash payments*	93.00

*As with the credit side of the cash book above, because there are a number of unlinked accounts which take the opposing entries, we have used a catch-all narrative under Details here (Petty cash payments).

Postage account

Details	£	Details	£
Petty cash	15.00		

Office cleaning account

Details	£	Details	£
Petty cash	30.00		

Stationery account

Details	£	Details	£
Petty cash	40.00		

VAT account

Details	£	Details	£
Petty cash	8.00		

A useful double check is that the new debit and credit postings in the ledger accounts balance each other out:

Ledger account	Debit entries £	Credit entries £
Petty cash		93.00
Postage	15.00	
Office cleaning	30.00	
Stationery	40.00	
VAT	8.00	
	93.00	93.00

The Petty Cash Book as part of the general ledger

As with the main cash book, in many businesses the Petty Cash Book is treated as **both** a book of prime entry **and** part of the general ledger. This means that the payments side of the Petty Cash Book is itself the credit side of a general ledger account (we saw in Chapter 7 that the debit side of the account is the Petty Cash Book for receipts).

The effect of this is that:

- There is no need to post a credit entry for the total column from the Petty Cash Book

- There is no petty cash or petty cash control account in the general ledger

- Debit entries for payments from the Petty Cash Book are posted as usual

CHAPTER OVERVIEW

- The first stage of the accounting process is to enter details of transactions into the books of prime entry eg Purchases and Purchases Returns Day Books and Cash Book

- The second stage is to transfer details from the books of prime entry to the accounting records ie the general ledger and purchases ledger

- The Purchases Day Book must be totalled and the totals entered into the ledger accounts in the general ledger

- Each individual purchase invoice must also be entered into the individual trade payable's account in the purchases ledger

- The Purchases Returns Day Book must also be totalled and posted to the general ledger and the purchases ledger

- The Cash Book must be totalled and posted to the general ledger

- Each cash payment in the purchases ledger column of the Cash Book must also be entered into the individual trade payable's account in the purchases ledger

- The discounts received column in the Cash Book must have both a debit and a credit posting in the general ledger

- The Petty Cash Book (credit side) must be totalled and posted to the petty cash or petty cash control account in the general ledger

Keywords

Purchases ledger control account – total trade payables account in the general ledger

Purchases ledger – collection of ledger accounts for individual credit suppliers (not part of the double entry system – a subsidiary ledger)

TEST YOUR LEARNING

Test 1

From the Purchases Day Book and Purchases Returns Day Book below, make the relevant entries in the general ledger and purchases ledger accounts.

Purchases Day Book

Date	Supplier	Invoice number	Supplier code	Invoice total £	VAT £	Net £
16/10	Herne Industries	46121	PL15	864.00	144.00	720.00
15/10	Bass Engineers	663211	PL13	460.80	76.80	384.00
12/10	Southfield Electrical	56521	PL20	2,008.80	334.80	1,674.00
				3,333.60	555.60	2,778.00

Purchases Returns Day Book

Date	Supplier	Credit note number	Supplier code	Credit note total £	VAT £	Net £
20/10	Southfield Electrical	08702	PL20	120.00	20.00	100.00
20/10	Herne Industries	4502	PL15	132.00	22.00	110.00
				252.00	42.00	210.00

General ledger

Purchases ledger control account

Details	£	Details	£

Purchases account

Details	£	Details	£

Purchases returns account

Details	£	Details	£

VAT account

Details	£	Details	£

Purchases ledger

Herne Industries   PL 15

Details	£	Details	£

Bass Engineers   PL 13

Details	£	Details	£

Southfield Electrical   PL 20

Details	£	Details	£

Test 2

Post from the Cash Book below to the general ledger and purchases ledger accounts. The Cash Book is **not** part of the double entry system.

Details	Ref	Bank £	VAT £	Discounts received £	Cash purchases £	Purchases ledger £	Sundry £
P Products Ltd	PL23	241.58				241.58	
Jason Bros	PL36	336.29		6.86		336.29	
P Taylor		255.24	42.54		212.70		
R R Partners	PL06	163.47		4.19		163.47	
Troyde Ltd	PL14	183.57				183.57	
O L Simms		119.40	19.90		99.50		
F Elliott	PL20	263.68		8.15		263.68	
G L Finance	GL400	200.00					200.00
		1,763.23	62.44	19.20	312.20	1,188.59	200.00

General ledger

VAT account — GL 100

Details	£	Details	£

Purchases account — GL 200

Details	£	Details	£

Purchases ledger control account — GL 300

Details	£	Details	£

Loan account — GL 400

Details	£	Details	£

Discounts received — GL 500

Details	£	Details	£

Bank — GL 600

Details	£	Details	£

Purchases ledger

R R Partners — PL 06

Details	£	Details	£

Troyde Ltd — PL 14

Details	£	Details	£

F Elliott   **PL 20**

Details	£	Details	£

P Products Ltd   **PL 23**

Details	£	Details	£

Jason Bros   **PL 36**

Details	£	Details	£

Test 3

The following transactions all took place on 30 November and have been entered into the purchases day book as shown below. No entries have yet been made into the ledger system.

Purchases day book

Date 20XX	Details	Invoice number	Total £	VAT @ 20% £	Net £
30 Nov	Lindell Co	24577	2,136	356	1,780
30 Nov	Harris Rugs	829	5,256	876	4,380
30 Nov	Kinshasa Music	10/235	2,796	466	2,330
30 Nov	Calnan Ltd	9836524	2,292	382	1,910
	Totals		12,480	2,080	10,400

Make the required entries in the general ledger.

VAT account

Details	£	Details	£

Purchases account

Details	£	Details	£

Purchases ledger control account

Details	£	Details	£

chapter 9:
INITIAL TRIAL BALANCE

chapter coverage 📖

Now that we have posted the books of prime entry to the general ledger, we complete this Text by extracting an initial trial balance, so we can be sure that the double entry is correct.

The topic covered is:

✎ Preparing a simple trial balance

THE TRIAL BALANCE

You will recall that in Chapter 6 we prepared and balanced the following ledger accounts for Ben Charles (remember we are now calling the trade receivables account the sales ledger control account, and the trade payables account the purchases ledger control account):

Bank account

Details	£	Details	£
Capital	10,000	Purchases	1,000
Sales	1,500	Rent	600
Sales ledger control	1,750	Non-current assets	1,000
		Stationery	200
		Drawings	500
		Purchases ledger control	1,500
		Balance c/d	8,450
	13,250		13,250
Balance b/d	8,450		

Capital account

Details	£	Details	£
		Bank	10,000

Purchases account

Details	£	Details	£
Bank	1,000		
Purchases ledger control	2,000	Balance c/d	3,000
	3,000		3,000
Balance b/d	3,000		

Purchases ledger control account

Details	£	Details	£
Bank	1,500	Purchases	2,000
Balance c/d	500		
	2,000		2,000
		Balance b/d	500

Rent account

Details	£	Details	£
Bank	600		

Sales account

Details	£	Details	£
		Bank	1,500
Balance c/d	3,300	Sales ledger control	1,800
	3,300		3,300
		Balance b/d	3,300

Sales ledger control account

Details	£	Details	£
Sales	1,800	Bank	1,750
		Discount allowed	50
	1,800		1,800

Non-current assets account

Details	£	Details	£
Bank	1,000		

Stationery account

Details	£	Details	£
Bank	200		

Drawings account

Details	£	Details	£
Bank	500		

Discounts allowed account

Details	£	Details	£
Sales ledger control	50		

Once all of the accounts have been balanced then a very useful exercise is often carried out. This is the preparation of an INITIAL TRIAL BALANCE.

The initial trial balance is simply a list of all of the debit and credit balances on each of the general ledger accounts. The purpose of the trial balance is that it forms a check on the accuracy of the entries in the ledger accounts. If the debits in the trial balance do not equal the credits then this indicates that there has been an error in the double entry.

HOW IT WORKS

Now we will complete Ben Charles's accounts for the period by preparing a trial balance.

Step 1   List the balance brought down on each account as a debit or credit as appropriate.

	Debits	Credits
	£	£
Bank	8,450	
Capital		10,000
Purchases	3,000	
Purchases ledger control		500
Rent	600	
Sales		3,300
Sales ledger control	0	
Non-current asset	1,000	
Stationery	200	
Drawings	500	
Discounts allowed	50	

Step 2 Total the debit column and the credit column and check that they are equal.

	Debits	Credits
	£	£
Bank	8,450	
Capital		10,000
Purchases	3,000	
Purchases ledger control		500
Rent	600	
Sales		3,300
Sales ledger control	0	
Non-current asset	1,000	
Stationery	200	
Drawings	500	
Discounts allowed	50	
	13,800	13,800

Task 1

You have been handed the completed general ledger accounts for Mr Chapter, whom we saw in Chapters 7 and 8. Note that:

- Balances brought forward from the previous period have been added to some of the accounts

- The two sides of the Bank account have been combined

- There is an additional account, for capital

Balance these accounts and produce an initial trial balance.

General ledger

Bank account

Details	£	Details	£
Balance (b/f)	15,000.00	Bank payments	6,816.00
Bank receipts	1,656.00		

Sales ledger control account

Details	£	Details	£
Balance (b/f)	10,000.00	Sales returns	274.00
Sales	1,730.00	Bank	1,416.00
		Discounts allowed	40.00

Sales account

Details	£	Details	£
		Balance b/f	20,000.00
		SLCA	1,450.00
		Bank	200.00

Sales returns account

Details	£	Details	£
SLCA	230.00		

VAT account

Details	£	Details	£
Sales returns	44.00	Balance b/f	1,500.00
Purchases	1,108.00	Sales	280.00
Bank	120.00	Bank	40.00
		Purchases returns	92.00

Discounts allowed account

Details	£	Details	£
SLCA	40.00		

Purchases ledger control account

Details	£	Details	£
Purchases returns	572.00	Balance b/f	2,500.00
Bank	6,096.00	Purchases	6,808.00
Discounts received	140.00		

Purchases account

Details	£	Details	£
PLCA	5,700.00		
Bank	600.00		

Purchases returns account

Details	£	Details	£
		PLCA	480.00

Discounts received account

Details	£	Details	£
		PLCA	140.00

Capital account

Details	£	Details	£
		Balance b/f	1,000.00

Trial balance

	Debits £	Credits £
Bank		
Sales ledger control		
Sales		
Sales returns		
VAT		
Discounts allowed		
Purchases ledger control		
Purchases		
Purchases returns		
Discounts received		
Capital		

BALANCES TO WATCH OUT FOR

When you are given a set of ledger accounts it is clear which side of the trial balance each balance should appear in: the same side as the balance brought down on the account.

However in your assessment you will be given a list of balances and required to identify from their names whether they are debit or credit balances. You should watch out for the following, which learners often get wrong:

Name of balance	Debit or credit balance?	Nature of balance
Inventory – of goods or materials held at any point in time	Debit	Asset
Bank overdraft	Credit	Liability
Cash at bank	Debit	Asset
Loan	Credit	Liability
VAT owed to HMRC	Credit	Liability
VAT owed by HMRC	Debit	Asset
Capital	Credit	Capital
Drawings	Debit	Reduction in capital
Bank interest paid or bank charges	Debit	Expense
Bank interest received	Credit	Income
Petty cash or petty cash control	Debit	Asset

CHAPTER OVERVIEW

- Ledger accounts are balanced by totalling both sides of the account, inserting the larger total at the bottom of both the debit and credit sides and putting in the figure that makes the smaller side of the account add back to this total. This is called the balance carried down and this balance is brought down on the other side of the account below the total

- A trial balance is prepared by listing all of the debit balances brought down and credit balances brought down and checking the total of these balances to ensure that they agree

Keyword

Initial trial balance – a list of all of the debit and credit balances brought down on the ledger accounts

TEST YOUR LEARNING

Test 1

Calculate and carry down the closing balances on each of the following accounts.

VAT account

	£		£
Purchases	3,778	Balance b/f	2,116
Bank	2,116	Sales	6,145

Sales account

	£		£
		Balance b/f	57,226
		SLCA	42,895

Sales ledger control account

	£		£
Balance b/f	4,689	Bank	21,505
Sales	23,512	Discounts allowed	2,019

Purchases ledger control account

	£		£
Purchases returns	1,334	Balance b/f	2,864
Bank	13,446	Purchases	14,552
Discounts received	662		

Test 2

Indicate whether each of the following balances would be shown as a debit balance or a credit balance in the trial balance.

	£	Debit balance ✓	Credit balance ✓
Discounts allowed	1,335		
Discounts received	1,013		
Purchases returns	4,175		
Sales returns	6,078		
Bank interest received	328		
Bank charges	163		

Test 3

Given below are the balances on the ledger accounts of Thames Traders at 30 November 20XX. Prepare the trial balance as at 30 November 20XX, including totals.

	£	Debits £	Credits £
Motor vehicles	64,000		
Office equipment	21,200		
Sales	238,000		
Purchases	164,000		
Bank overdraft	1,080		
Petty cash control	30		
Capital	55,000		
Sales returns	4,700		
Purchases returns	3,600		
Sales ledger control	35,800		
Purchases ledger control	30,100		
VAT (owed to HMRC)	12,950		
Telephone	1,600		
Electricity	2,800		
Wages	62,100		
Loan from bank	30,000		
Discounts allowed	6,400		
Discounts received	3,900		
Rent expense	12,000		
Totals			

Test 4

Below is a list of balances to be transferred to the trial balance as at 30 June.

Place the figures in the debit or credit column, as appropriate, and total each column.

Account name	Amount £	Debit £	Credit £
Advertising	3,238		
Bank overdraft	27,511		
Capital	40,846		
Discount allowed	4,416		
Discount received	2,880		
Hotel expenses	2,938		
Loan from bank	39,600		
Miscellaneous expenses	3,989		
Motor expenses	7,087		
Motor vehicles	63,120		
Petty cash control	720		
Purchases	634,529		
Purchases ledger control	110,846		
Purchases returns	1,618		
Rent and rates	19,200		
Sales	1,051,687		
Sales ledger control	405,689		
Sales returns	11,184		
Stationery	5,880		
Inventory	46,668		
Subscriptions	864		
Telephone	3,838		
VAT owing to HM Revenue & Customs	63,650		
Wages	125,278		
Totals			

ANSWERS TO CHAPTER TASKS

CHAPTER 1 Business documentation

1   a credit transaction   ✓

2   an invoice   ✓

3   a credit note   ✓

4   a remittance advice note   ✓

5   a petty cash voucher   ✓

6   PRE62   ✓

CHAPTER 2   Discounts and VAT

1

Output tax is VAT on	sales
Input tax is VAT on	purchases

2   £230 × 20/100 = £46

£	46

3   £246 × 20/120 = £41.00

£	41

4

	£
List price	2,400.00
Less: discount £2,400.00 × 15/100	(360.00)
	2,040.00
VAT: £2,040.00 × 20/100	408.00
	2,448.00

£	2,448.00

5

	£
List price	2,400.00
Less: trade discount £2,400.00 × 10/100	(240.00)
	2,160.00
Less: bulk discount £2,160.00 × 12/100	(259.20)
	1,900.80
VAT: £1,900.80 × 20/100	380.16
	2,280.96

£	**2,280.96**

6

	£
Net total	368.00
Less: settlement discount	(11.04)
	356.96
Net total	368.00
VAT £356.96 × 20/100 (rounded down)	71.39
Invoice total	439.39

£	**439.39**

CHAPTER 3   The basics of accounting

1

	£	Invoice total	VAT	Net
Goods total	1,236.00			✓
VAT	247.20		✓	
Total	1,483.20	✓		

2

An invoice is entered on the	left	side of the customer's account
A credit note is entered on the	right	side of the customer's account

£	**24.00**

3

Invoice total £	VAT £	Net £	Computers £	Printers £	Scanners £
1,560.00	260.00	1,300.00	800.00	300.00	200.00

4

An invoice is entered on the	right	side of the supplier's account
A credit note is entered on the	left	side of the supplier's account

£	36.00

5

Invoice total £	VAT £	Net £	Purchases £	Expenses £
1,980.00	330.00	1,650.00	1,650.00	

6

True	✓
False	

7

£	0.00

8

On any payments that are not payments to credit suppliers (trade payables) ✓

9

£	0.00

CHAPTER 4   Accounting for credit sales

1

The buyer of goods

2

Yes

Working: £400 × 95% = £380 + £76 (VAT) = <u>£456</u>

CHAPTER 5   Accounting for credit purchases

1

£	304

Working

	£
Net total	1,600.00
Less discount 5/100 × £1,600	(80.00)
	1,520.00
VAT £1,520.00 × 20/100	304.00

2   Discount = £800.00 × 3/100 =

£	24

3

5 August

Working

(9 + 30 – 3 – 31)

4

1 December

Working

(23 + 10 – 2 – 30)

5

£	2,340

Working

£2,390 – (2.5/100 × £2,000)

CHAPTER 6   Double entry bookkeeping

1

(a) Purchase of goods on credit

Increase expense	✓
Increase sales	
Increase trade payable	✓
Increase trade receivable	

(b) Sale of goods on credit

Increase expense	
Increase sales	✓
Increase trade payable	
Increase trade receivable	✓

(c) Receipt of money for sale of goods on credit

Increase cash	✓
Decrease cash	
Decrease trade receivable	✓
Increase trade receivable	

(d) Payment to a trade payable for purchase of goods on credit

Increase cash	
Decrease cash	✓
Decrease trade payable	✓
Increase trade payable	

2

(a) Purchase of goods on credit

Account name	Debit	Credit
Purchases	✓	
Trade payables		✓

(b) Sale of goods on credit

Account name	Debit	Credit
Trade receivables	✓	
Sales		✓

(c) Receipt of money for sale of goods on credit

Account name	Debit	Credit
Bank	✓	
Trade receivables		✓

(d) Payment of a trade payable

Account name	Debit	Credit
Trade payables	✓	
Bank		✓

3

Trade receivables			
Details	**£**	**Details**	**£**
Sales	2,600	Bank	1,800
Sales	1,400	Bank	1,200
Sales	3,700	Bank	2,000
Sales	1,300	Balance c/d	4,000
Total	9,000	Total	9,000
Balance b/d	4,000		

What does the balance represent?

The amount owed by trade receivables	✓
The amount owed to trade receivables	

4

	Revenue expenditure	Revenue income	Capital expenditure	Capital income
Sale of goods to credit customers		✓		
Cash sales		✓		
Sale of van				✓
Purchase of goods for resale	✓			
Purchase of building			✓	
Purchase of coffee for office from petty cash	✓			

5

James Daniels

	£		£
SDB	1,000	CB	800

CHAPTER 7 Double entry for sales and trade receivables

1

	Account name	Debit	Credit
Invoice total	Sales ledger control	✓	
VAT	VAT		✓
Net	Sales		✓

2

	Amount £	Debit	Credit
Sales ledger control account (general ledger)	240		✓
Customer's account (sales ledger)	240		✓

3

Sales Day Book

Customer	Invoice number	Customer code	Invoice total £	VAT £	Net £
Trissom Ltd	124	SL 09	1,190.00	190.00	1,000.00
Miley & Co	125	SL 22	540.00	90.00	450.00
Totals			1,730.00	280.00	1,450.00

Sales Returns Day Book

Customer	Credit note number	Customer code	Credit note total £	VAT £	Net £
Trissom Ltd	07	SL 09	238.00	38.00	200.00
Miley & Co	08	SL 22	36.00	6.00	30.00
Totals			274.00	44.00	230.00

Cash Book

Details	Ref	Bank £	VAT £	Discounts allowed £	Cash sales £	Sales ledger £	Other £
Trissom Ltd	SL 09	912.00		40.00		912.00	
Miley & Co	SL 22	504.00				504.00	
Cash sale		240.00	40.00		200.00		
Totals		1,656.00	40.00	40.00	200.00	1,416.00	

General ledger

Bank account

Details	£	Details	£
Bank receipts	1,656.00		

Sales ledger control account

Details	£	Details	£
Sales	1,730.00	Sales returns	274.00
		Bank	1,416.00
		Discounts allowed	40.00

Sales account			
Details	£	Details	£
		SLCA	1,450.00
		Bank	200.00

Sales returns account

Details	£	Details	£
SLCA	230.00		

VAT account

Details	£	Details	£
Sales returns	44.00	Sales	280.00
		Bank	40.00

Discounts allowed account

Details	£	Details	£
SLCA	40.00		

Sales ledger

Trissom Ltd — SL 09

Details	£	Details	£
SDB – 124	1,190.00	SRDB – CN07	238.00
		CB – cash	912.00
		CB – discounts allowed	40.00

Miley & Co — SL 22

Details	£	Details	£
SDB – 125	540.00	SRDB – CN08	36.00
		CB – cash	504.00

4

Account name	Amount £	Debit ✓	Credit ✓
VAT	20.00		✓
Sales	100.00		✓
Sales ledger control account	65.00		✓
Sales ledger control account	5,116.50		✓
Discounts allowed	65.00	✓	

Remember that the 'Bank' column in the cash book is acting as the debit side of the Bank account in the general ledger, so no additional debit posting is required.

CHAPTER 8 Double entry for purchases and trade payables

1

	Account name	Debit ✓	Credit ✓
Invoice total	Purchases ledger control		✓
VAT	VAT	✓	
Purchases	Purchases	✓	

2

	Amount £	Debit ✓	Credit ✓
Purchases ledger control account (general ledger)	720	✓	
Supplier's account (purchases ledger)	720	✓	

3

Purchases Day Book

Supplier	Invoice number	Supplier code	Invoice total £	VAT £	Net £
Rawley Ltd	7869	PL54	3,000.00	500.00	2,500.00
Jipsum plc	323980	PL02	3,808.00	608.00	3,200.00
Totals			6,808.00	1,108.00	5,700.00

Purchases Returns Day Book

Customer	Credit note number	Customer code	Credit note total £	VAT £	Net £
Rawley Ltd	CN627	PL54	96.00	16.00	80.00
Jipsum plc	CN08	PL02	476.00	76.00	400.00
Totals			572.00	92.00	480.00

Cash Book

Details	Ref	Bank £	VAT £	Discounts received £	Cash purchases £	Purchases ledger £
Rawley Ltd	PL54	2,904.00				2,904.00
Jipsum plc	PL02	3,192.00		140.00		3,192.00
Cash purchase		720.00	120.00		600.00	
Totals		6,816.00	120.00	140.00	600.00	6,096.00

General ledger

Bank account

Details	£	Details	£
		Bank payments	6,816.00

Purchases ledger control account

Details	£	Details	£
Purchases returns	572.00	Purchases	6,808.00
Bank	6,096.00		
Discounts received	140.00		

Purchases account

Details	£	Details	£
PLCA	5,700.00		
Bank	600.00		

Purchases returns account

Details	£	Details	£
		PLCA	480.00

VAT account

Details	£	Details	£
Purchases	1,108.00	Purchases returns	92.00
Bank	120.00		

Discounts received account

Details	£	Details	£
		PLCA	140.00

Purchases ledger

Rawley Ltd PL 54

Details	£	Details	£
PRDB – CN627	96.00	PDB – 7869	3,000.00
CB	2,904.00		

Jipsum plc PL 02

Details	£	Details	£
PRDB – CN08	476.00	PDB – 323980	3,808.00
CB – cash	3,192.00		
CB – discount	140.00		

4

Account name	Amount £	Debit ✓	Credit ✓
VAT	48.00	✓	
Purchases	240.00	✓	
Purchases ledger control account	109.00	✓	
Purchases ledger control account	3,009.65	✓	
Discounts received	109.00		✓

Remember that the 'Bank' column in the Cash Payments Book is acting as the credit side of the Bank account in the general ledger, so no additional credit posting is required.

CHAPTER 9   Initial trial balance

1

Bank account

Details	£	Details	£
Balance brought down (b/d)	15,000.00	Bank payments	6,816.00
Bank receipts	1,656.00	Balance carried down (c/d)	9,840.00
	16,656.00		16,656.00
Balance b/d	9,840.00		

Sales ledger control account

Details	£	Details	£
Balance b/d	10,000.00	Sales returns	274.00
Sales	1,730.00	Bank	1,416.00
		Discounts allowed	40.00
		Balance c/d	10,000.00
	11,730.00		11,730.00
Balance b/d	10,000.00		

Sales account

Details	£	Details	£
		Balance b/d	20,000.00
		SLCA	1,450.00
Balance c/d	21,650.00	Bank	200.00
	21,650.00		21,650.00
		Balance b/d	21,650.00

Sales returns account

Details	£	Details	£
SLCA	230.00		

VAT account

Details	£	Details	£
Sales returns	44.00	Balance b/d	1,500.00
Purchases	1,108.00	Sales	280.00
Bank	120.00	Bank	40.00
Balance c/d	640.00	Purchases returns	92.00
	1,912.00		1,912.00
		Balance b/d	640.00

Discounts allowed account

Details	£	Details	£
SLCA	40.00		

Purchases ledger control account

Details	£	Details	£
Purchases returns	572.00	Balance b/d	2,500.00
Bank	6,096.00	Purchases	6,808.00
Discounts received	140.00		
Balance c/d	2,500.00		
	9,308.00		9,308.00
		Balance b/d	2,500.00

Purchases account

Details	£	Details	£
PLCA	5,700.00		
Bank	600.00	Balance c/d	6,300.00
	6,300.00		6,300.00
Balance b/d	6,300.00		

Purchases returns account

Details	£	Details	£
		PLCA	480.00

Discounts received account

Details	£	Details	£
		PLCA	140.00

Capital account

Details	£	Details	£
		Balance b/d	1,000.00

Trial balance

	Debits £	Credits £
Bank	9,840.00	
Sales ledger control	10,000.00	
Sales		21,650.00
Sales returns	230.00	
VAT		640.00
Discounts allowed	40.00	
Purchases ledger control		2,500.00
Purchases	6,300.00	
Purchases returns		480.00
Discounts received		140.00
Capital		1,000.00
	26,410.00	26,410.00

TEST YOUR LEARNING – ANSWERS

CHAPTER 1   Business documentation

1

	Cash ✓	Credit ✓
Purchase of a van with an agreed payment date in one month's time		✓
Sale of goods by credit card in a shop	✓	
Purchase of computer disks by cheque	✓	
Purchase of computer disks which are accompanied by an invoice		✓
Sale of goods which are paid for by cheque	✓	

2

Sale of goods for cash	Till receipt
Return of goods purchased on credit	Credit note
Reimbursement of employee for expense by cash	Petty cash voucher
Indication of which amounts that are owed are being paid	Remittance advice note

3

- Where income is more than expenses a business makes a profit

- Where expenses are more than income a business makes a loss

- Bank loans and overdrafts are examples of liabilities

- Cash and receivables are examples of assets

- When a business owner contributes money to the business, this is known as capital

- When a business owner takes out money from the business, this is known as drawings

CHAPTER 2   Discounts and VAT

1   (400 × 30) – (400 × 30 × 5/100) = £11,400 before bulk discount

11,400 – (11,400 × 10/100) = £10,260 net amount after bulk discount

£	10,260

2   (a)   VAT   =   £378.00 × 20% (20/100)

£	75.60

(b)   VAT   =   £378.00 × 20/120

£	63.00

Net amount   =   £378.00 – 63.00

£	315.00

3   (a)   VAT   =   £3,154.80 × 20/120 = £525.80

Net amount   =   £3,154.80 – 525.80 = £2,629.00

(b)   VAT   =   £446.40 × 20/120 = £74.40

Net amount   =   £446.40 – 74.40   = £372.00

(c)   VAT   =   £169.20 × 20/120 = £28.20

Net amount   =   £169.20 – 28.20   = £141.00

VAT-inclusive amount	VAT	Net amount
(a) £3,154.80	£525.80	£2,629.00
(b) £446.40	£74.40	£372.00
(c) £169.20	£28.20	£141.00

4   (a)

(i) Total cost before discount	23 × £56.00	£1,288.00
(ii) Discount	15% × £1,288.00	£193.20
(iii) Net total	£1,288.00 – £193.20	£1,094.80
(iv) VAT	20% × £1,094.80	£218.96
(v) Invoice total		£1,313.76

(b)

(i) Total cost before discount	23 × £56.00	£1,288.00
(ii) Discount	15% × £1,288.00	£193.20
(iii) Net total		£1,094.80
(iv) VAT	20% × (1,094.80 – (3% × 1,094.80))	£212.39
(v) Invoice total		£1,307.19

CHAPTER 3   The basics of accounting

1   Sales Day Book

Date	Customer	Invoice number	Customer code	Invoice total £	VAT (Net × 20%) £	Net £
1/6	J Jepson	44263	SL34	141.60	23.60	118.00
2/6	S Beck & Sons	44264	SL01	384.00	64.00	320.00
3/6	Penfold Ltd	44265	SL23	196.80	32.80	164.00
4/6	S Beck & Sons	44266	SL01	307.20	51.20	256.00
4/6	J Jepson	44267	SL34	172.80	28.80	144.00
Total				1,202.40	200.40	1,002.00

Sales Returns Day Book

Date	Customer	Credit note number	Customer code	Credit note total £	VAT (Net × 20%) £	Net £
2/6	Scroll Ltd	3813	SL16	21.60	3.60	18.00
5/6	Penfold Ltd	3814	SL23	20.16	3.36	16.80
Total				41.76	6.96	34.80

2 Purchases Day Book

Date	Supplier	Invoice number	Supplier code	Invoice total £	VAT £	Net £
6/6	YH Hill	224363	PL16	190.08	31.68	158.40
6/6	Letra Ltd	PT445	PL24	273.60	45.60	228.00
6/6	Coldstores Ltd	77352	PL03	189.60	31.60	158.00
Total				653.28	108.88	544.40

Purchases Returns Day Book

Date	Supplier	Credit note number	Supplier code	Credit note total £	VAT £	Net £
6/6	Letra Ltd	CN92	PL24	120.00	20.00	100.00
6/6	YH Hill	C7325	PL16	31.20	5.20	26.00
Total				151.20	25.20	126.00

3

Cash Book – receipts

Date	Details	Ref	Bank £	VAT £	Disc allowed £	Cash sales £	Sales ledger £	Sundry £
1/6	J Jepson	SL34	220.00		10.00		220.00	
3/6	Cash sale		72.00	12.00		60.00		

Cash Book – payments

Date	Details	Ref	Bank £	VAT £	Disc received £	Cash purchases £	Purchases ledger £	Petty cash £	Su
3/6	Letra Ltd	PL24	500.00		20.00		500.00		
2/6	Cash purchase		48.00	8.00		40.00			

CHAPTER 4   Accounting for credit sales

1

To inform the customer of the amount due for a sale	Invoice
To inform the seller of the quantities required	Customer purchase order
To inform the seller that some of the delivery was not of the standard or type required	Returns note
To inform the customer of the quantity delivered	Delivery note
To inform the customer that the invoiced amount was overstated	Credit note

2   (a)

	£
Cost before discount 23 × £56.00	1,288.00
Trade discount 15% × £1,288.00	(193.20)
Net of discount price	1,094.80
VAT 20% × £1,094.80	218.96
Total cost	1,313.76

(b)

	£
Cost before discount 23 × £56.00	1,288.00
Trade discount 15% × £1,288.00	(193.20)
Net of discount price	1,094.80
VAT 20% × (1,094.80 – (3% × 1,094.80))	212.39
or 1,094.80 × 0.97 × 0.2	
Total cost	1,307.19

3   Errors on the invoice:

- It is not dated
- There is no customer code
- The calculation of the total cost of the tumble dryers is incorrect

- The calculation of the trade discount is incorrect
- The VAT has been calculated without taking account of the settlement discount offered

Corrected figures:

	£
Tumble dryers 21 × £180	3,780.00
Mixers	400.00
Goods total	4,180.00
Less: 15% discount	(627.00)
Net total	3,553.00
VAT 20% × (3,553 – (5% × 3,553))	675.07
Invoice total	4,228.07

4 (a) and (b)

Date	Customer	Invoice number	Customer code	Invoice total £	VAT £	Net £
21/9	Dagwell Enterprises	56401	SL 15	948.60	158.10	790.50
21/9	G Thomas & Co	56402	SL 30	3,514.01	566.01	2,948.00
22/9	Polygon Stores	56403	SL 03	1,965.60	327.60	1,638.00
23/9	Weller Enterprises	56404	SL 18	1,144.32	184.32	960.00
	Totals			7,572.53	1,236.03	6,336.50

5 Cheque from Quinn Ltd – the remittance advice has been correctly cast but there has been an error made in writing the cheque as the cheque is for £770.80 rather than £770.08.

Cheque from T T Peters – the remittance advice has been incorrectly cast and the cheque total should have been for £1,191.02.

6 By a process of trial and error you can find the invoices and credit note that total to £226.79.

Invoice/credit note number	£
30234	157.35
30239	85.24
CN2381	(15.80)
Total	226.79

7 Sales ledger

Account name	Amount £	Left side of account ✓	Right side of account ✓	Details in account
Fries & Co	2,136	✓		SDB - 23907
Hussey Enterprises	3,108	✓		SDB – 23908
Todd Trading	3,720	✓		SDB – 23909
Milford Ltd	2,592	✓		SDB - 23910

8 Sales Day Book

Date 20XX	Details	Invoice number	Total £	VAT @ 20% £	Net £	Sales type 1 £	Sales type 2 £
30 Nov	Wright & Co	5627	12,000	2,000	10,000	10,000	
30 Nov	H Topping	5628	1,560	260	1,300		1,300
30 Nov	Sage Ltd	5629	600	100	500	500	
	Totals		14,160	2,360	11,800	10,500	1,300

9

<table>
<tr><td colspan="6" align="center">**Wendlehurst Trading**
VAT Registration No. 876983479</td></tr>
<tr><td colspan="3">Stroll In Stores</td><td colspan="3">Customer account code: ST725
Delivery note number: 8973
Date: 1 Dec 20XX</td></tr>
<tr><td colspan="6" align="center">**Invoice No: 624**</td></tr>
<tr><td>Quantity of cases</td><td>Product code</td><td>Total list price £</td><td>Net amount after discount £</td><td>VAT £</td><td>Gross £</td></tr>
<tr><td>600/12 = 50</td><td>TIG300</td><td>500.00</td><td>425.00</td><td>81.60</td><td>506.60</td></tr>
</table>

10

<table>
<tr><td colspan="4" align="center">**Wendlehurst Trading**
VAT Registration No. 876983479</td></tr>
<tr><td colspan="4">To: Holroyda
Date: 30 Nov 20XX</td></tr>
<tr><td>Date 20XX</td><td>Details</td><td>Transaction amount £</td><td>Outstanding amount £</td></tr>
<tr><td>18 Nov</td><td>Invoice 5607</td><td>4,390</td><td>4,390</td></tr>
<tr><td>21 Nov</td><td>Invoice 5612</td><td>1,400</td><td>5,790</td></tr>
<tr><td>22 Nov</td><td>Credit note 524</td><td>160</td><td>5,630</td></tr>
<tr><td>29 Nov</td><td>Invoice 5616</td><td>980</td><td>6,610</td></tr>
<tr><td>30 Nov</td><td>Payment received – thank you</td><td>−4,000</td><td>2,610</td></tr>
</table>

CHAPTER 5   Accounting for credit purchases

1

To accompany goods being returned to a supplier .	Returns note
To record for internal purposes the quantity of goods received	Goods received note
To request payment from a purchaser of goods	Invoice
To order goods from a supplier	Purchase order
To accompany payment to a supplier	Remittance advice note

2 If an order is placed over the telephone then the immediate problem is that there is no documentary evidence for that order. Some form of documentary evidence will be required when the goods are received, in order to check that they were actually ordered, and when the invoice is received to check that it is for the correct quantity. This can be solved ideally by requesting a confirmation of the order from the supplier. If that is not possible then a written note of all of the order details should be made and filed.

3 ▪ The invoice does not agree to the purchase order as only 70 Get Well cards were ordered. However when the credit note is taken into account the invoice quantity is correct minus the credit note quantity

  ▪ The unit price on the credit note is only £0.25 whereas the invoice price is £0.33

4

Purchases Day Book

Date	Supplier	Invoice number	Supplier code	Invoice total £	VAT £	Net £
16/10	Herne Industries	46121	PL15	864.00	144.00	720.00
15/10	Bass Engineers	663211	PL13	460.80	76.80	384.00
12/10	Southfield Electrical	56521	PL20	1,995.40	321.40	1,674.00
	Total			3,320.20	542.20	2,778.00

5

Purchases Returns Day Book

Date	Supplier	Credit note number	Supplier code	Credit note total £	VAT £	Net £
16/10	Southfield Electrical	08702	PL20	120.00	20.00	100.00
17/10	Herne Industries	4502	PL15	132.00	22.00	110.00
	Total			252.00	42.00	210.00

6

REMITTANCE ADVICE

To:
Fishpool Supplies
280, Main Rd
Winnish DR2 5TL

From:
Tryprint Traders
Barnsgate Ind Park
Fretton PT7 2XY

Invoice	Amount £
61234	401.23
61287	226.40
61299	106.68
CN 4361	(16.48)

Cheque enclosed £ 717.83

7   **Purchases ledger**

Account name	Amount £	Left side of account ✓	Right side of account ✓	Details in account
Lindell Co	2,136		✓	PDB 24577
Harris Rugs	5,256		✓	PDB 829
Kinshasa Music	2,796		✓	PDB 10/235
Calnan Ltd	2,292		✓	PDB 9836524

8   **Purchases Day Book**

Date 20XX	Details	Invoice number	Total £	VAT @ 20% £	Net £	Purchases £	Expenses £
30 Nov	Papford & Co	29000	3,180	530	2,650		2,650
30 Nov	Havelock Beauty	120/22	1,176	196	980	980	
30 Nov	Hareston Ltd	7638	9,384	1,564	7,820	7,820	
	Totals		13,740	2,290	11,450	8,800	2,650

9

	Yes ✓	No ✓
Has the correct purchase price of the printer paper been charged?	✓	
Has the correct trade discount been applied?		✓
What would be the VAT amount charged if the invoice was correct?	£	70.00
What would be the total amount charged if the invoice was correct?	£	420.00

CHAPTER 6   Double entry bookkeeping

1

	Debit	Credit
Money paid into the business by the owner	Bank	Capital
Purchases on credit	Purchases	Purchases ledger control
Purchases of machinery for use in the business, paid for by cheque	Non-current asset	Bank
Sales on credit	Sales ledger control	Sales
Money taken out of the business by the owner	Drawings	Bank

2

Sales ledger control

Date	Details	Amount £	Date	Details	Amount £
1/6	Balance b/d	1,209	28/6	Bank	3,287
30/6	Sales	6,298	30/6	Sales returns	786
			30/6	Balance c/d	3,434
	Total	7,507		Total	7,507
1/7	Balance b/d	3,434			

3   General ledger

Account name	Amount £	Debit ✓	Credit ✓	Details in account
Sales	9,630		✓	SLCA
VAT	1,926		✓	Sales
Sales ledger control	11,556	✓		Sales

4   General ledger

Account name	Amount £	Debit ✓	Credit ✓	Details in account
Purchases	10,400	✓		PLCA
VAT	2,080	✓		Purchases
Purchases ledger control	12,480		✓	Purchases

CHAPTER 7   Double entry for sales and receivables

1

General ledger

Sales ledger control account

Details	£	Details	£
Sales	7,603.80	Sales returns	601.20

Sales account

Details	£	Details	£
		SLCA	6,336.50

Sales returns account

Details	£	Details	£
SLCA	501.00		

VAT account

Details	£	Details	£
Sales returns	100.20	Sales	1,267.30

Sales ledger

Dagwell Enterprises   SL 15

Details	£	Details	£
SDB – Invoice 56401	948.60	SRDB – Credit note 08651	244.80

G Thomas & Co — SL 30

Details	£	Details	£
SDB – Invoice 56402	3,537.60		

Polygon Stores — SL 03

Details	£	Details	£
SDB – Invoice 56403	1,965.60		

Weller Enterprises — SL 18

Details	£	Details	£
SDB – Invoice 56404	1,152.00		

Whitehill Superstores — SL 37

Details	£	Details	£
		SRDB – Credit note 08650	356.40

2

General ledger

VAT account — GL 562

Details	£	Details	£
		Bank	112.12

Sales account — GL 049

Details	£	Details	£
		Bank	560.64

Sales ledger control account — GL 827

Details	£	Details	£
		Bank	981.12
		Discounts allowed	10.40

Discounts allowed account — GL 235

Details	£	Details	£
SLCA	10.40		

Sales ledger

		H Henry	**SL 0115**
Details	£	Details	£
		CB	146.79

		P Peters	**SL 0135**
Details	£	Details	£
		CB	221.55
		CB – discount	6.85

		K Kilpin	**SL 0128**
Details	£	Details	£
		CB	440.30

		B Bennet	**SL 0134**
Details	£	Details	£
		CB	57.80

		S Shahir	**SL 0106**
Details	£	Details	£
		CB	114.68
		CB – discount	3.55

3

General ledger

		Bank	**GL 100**
Details	£	Details	£
Bank receipts	2,702.67		

		VAT account	**GL 710**
Details	£	Details	£
		Bank	168.15

Sales account GL 110

Details	£	Details	£
		Bank	840.75

Sales ledger control account GL 560

Details	£	Details	£
		Bank	1,693.77
		Discounts allowed	63.30

Discounts allowed account GL 280

Details	£	Details	£
SLCA	63.30		

Sales ledger

G Gonpipe SL 55

Details	£	Details	£
		CB	332.67

J Jimmings SL 04

Details	£	Details	£
		CB	127.37
		CB – discount	6.70

N Nutely SL 16

Details	£	Details	£
		CB	336.28
		CB – discounts	17.70

T Turner SL 21

Details	£	Details	£
		CB	158.35

R Ritner SL 45

Details	£	Details	£
		CB	739.10
		CB – discount	38.90

4

VAT account

Details	£	Details	£
		Sales	1,926

Sales account

Details	£	Details	£
		SLCA	9,630

Sales ledger control account

Details	£	Details	£
Sales	11,556		

CHAPTER 8   Double entry for purchases and payables

1

General ledger

Purchases ledger control account

Details	£	Details	£
Purchases returns	252.00	Purchases	3,333.60

Purchases account

Details	£	Details	£
PLCA	2,778.00		

Purchases returns account

Details	£	Details	£
		PLCA	210.00

VAT account

Details	£	Details	£
Purchases	555.60	Purchases returns	42.00

BPP
LEARNING MEDIA

Purchases ledger

Herne Industries — PL 15

Details	£	Details	£
Credit note 4502	132.00	Invoice 46121	864.00

Bass Engineers — PL 13

Details	£	Details	£
		Invoice 663211	460.80

Southfield Electrical — PL 20

Details	£	Details	£
Credit note 08702	120.00	Invoice 56521	2,008.80

2

General ledger

VAT account — GL 100

Details	£	Details	£
Bank	62.44		

Purchases account — GL 200

Details	£	Details	£
Bank	312.20		

Purchases ledger control account — GL 300

Details	£	Details	£
Bank	1,188.59		
Discounts received	19.20		

Loan account — GL 400

Details	£	Details	£
Bank	200.00		

Discounts received GL 500

Details	£	Details	£
		PLCA	19.20

Bank GL 600

Details	£	Details	£
		Bank payments	1,763.23

Purchases ledger

R R Partners PL 06

Details	£	Details	£
CB	163.47		
CB – discount	4.19		

Troyde Ltd PL 14

Details	£	Details	£
CB	183.57		

F Elliott PL 20

Details	£	Details	£
CB	263.68		
CB – discount	8.15		

P Products Ltd PL 23

Details	£	Details	£
CB	241.58		

Jason Bros PL 36

Details	£	Details	£
CB	336.29		
CB – discount	6.86		

3

VAT account

Details	£	Details	£
Purchases	2,080.00		

Purchases account

Details	£	Details	£
PLCA	10,400.00		

Purchases ledger control account

Details	£	Details	£
		Purchases	12,480.00

CHAPTER 9   Initial trial balance

1

VAT account

Details	£	Details	£
Purchases	3,778	Balance b/f	2,116
Bank	2,116	Sales	6,145
Balance c/d	2,367		
	8,261		8,261
		Balance b/d	2,367

Sales account

Details	£	Details	£
		Balance b/f	57,226
Balance c/d	100,121	SLCA	42,895
	100,121		100,121
		Balance b/d	100,121

Sales ledger control account

Details	£	Details	£
Balance b/f	4,689	Bank	21,505
Sales	23,512	Discounts allowed	2,019
		Balance c/d	4,677
	28,201		28,201
Balance b/d	4,677		

Purchases ledger control account

Details	£	Details	£
Purchases returns	1,334	Balance b/f	2,864
Bank	13,446	Purchases	14,552
Discounts received	662		
Balance c/d	1,974		
	17,416		17,416
		Balance b/d	1,974

2

	£	Debit balance ✓	Credit balance ✓
Discounts allowed	1,335	✓	
Discounts received	1,013		✓
Purchases returns	4,175		✓
Sales returns	6,078	✓	
Bank interest received	328		✓
Bank charges	163	✓	

3

	Debits £	Credits £
Motor vehicles	64,000	
Office equipment	21,200	
Sales		238,000
Purchases	164,000	
Bank overdraft		1,080
Petty cash control	30	
Capital		55,000
Sales returns	4,700	
Purchases returns		3,600
Sales ledger control	35,800	
Purchases ledger control		30,100
VAT (owed to HMRC)		12,950
Telephone	1,600	
Electricity	2,800	
Wages	62,100	
Loan from bank		30,000
Discounts allowed	6,400	
Discounts received		3,900
Rent expense	12,000	
Totals	374,630	374,630

4

Account name	Amount £	Debit £	Credit £
Advertising	3,238	3,238	
Bank overdraft	27,511		27,511
Capital	40,846		40,846
Discount allowed	4,416	4,416	
Discount received	2,880		2,880
Hotel expenses	2,938	2,938	
Inventory	46,668	46,668	
Loan from bank	39,600		39,600
Miscellaneous expenses	3,989	3,989	
Motor expenses	7,087	7,087	
Motor vehicles	63,120	63,120	
Petty cash control	720	720	
Purchases	634,529	634,529	
Purchases ledger control	110,846		110,846
Purchases returns	1,618		1,618
Rent and rates	19,200	19,200	
Sales	1,051,687		1,051,687
Sales ledger control	405,689	405,689	
Sales returns	11,184	11,184	
Stationery	5,880	5,880	
Inventory	46,668		
Subscriptions	864	864	
Telephone	3,838	3,838	
VAT owing to HM Revenue & Customs	63,650		63,650
Wages	125,278	125,278	
Totals		1,338,638	1,338,638

INDEX

Notes

Notes

Notes

REVIEW FORM

How have you used this Text?
(Tick one box only)

☐ Home study

☐ On a course_____

☐ Other _____

Why did you decide to purchase this Text?
(Tick one box only)

☐ Have used BPP Texts in the past

☐ Recommendation by friend/colleague

☐ Recommendation by a college lecturer

☐ Saw advertising

☐ Other _____

During the past six months do you recall seeing/receiving either of the following?
(Tick as many boxes as are relevant)

☐ Our advertisement in Accounting Technician

☐ Our Publishing Catalogue

Which (if any) aspects of our advertising do you think are useful?
(Tick as many boxes as are relevant)

☐ Prices and publication dates of new editions

☐ Information on Text content

☐ Details of our free online offering

☐ None of the above

Your ratings, comments and suggestions would be appreciated on the following areas of this Text.

	Very useful	Useful	Not useful
Introductory section	☐	☐	☐
Quality of explanations	☐	☐	☐
How it works	☐	☐	☐
Chapter tasks	☐	☐	☐
Chapter overviews	☐	☐	☐
Test your learning	☐	☐	☐
Index	☐	☐	☐

	Excellent	Good	Adequate	Poor
Overall opinion of this Text	☐	☐	☐	☐

Do you intend to continue using BPP Products? ☐ Yes ☐ No

Please note any further comments and suggestions/errors on the reverse of this page. The author of this edition can be e-mailed at: paulsutcliffe@bpp.com

Please return to: Paul Sutcliffe, Senior Publishing Manager, **BPP Learning Media Ltd, FREEPOST, London, W12 8BR.**

REVIEW FORM (continued)

TELL US WHAT YOU THINK

Please note any further comments and suggestions/errors below.